GOD, FAITH,

⸙ *and* ⸙

REASON

GOD, FAITH,

❦ *and* ❧

REASON

MICHAEL SAVAGE

CENTER
STREET®

NEW YORK   NASHVILLE

Center Street
Hachette Book Group
1290 Avenue of the Americas, New York, NY 10104
centerstreet.com
twitter.com/centerstreet

First Edition: November 2017

Center Street is a division of Hachette Book Group, Inc. The Center Street name and logo are trademarks of Hachette Book Group, Inc.

The publisher is not responsible for websites (or their content) that are not owned by the publisher.

The Hachette Speakers Bureau provides a wide range of authors for speaking events. To find out more, go to www.HachetteSpeakersBureau.com or call (866) 376-6591.

Print book interior design by Timothy Shaner, NightandDayDesign.biz

Library of Congress Cataloging-in-Publication Data has been applied for.

ISBNs: 978-1-4789-7671-4 (hardcover), 978-1-5460-8245-3 (large type), 978-1-5460-8267-5 (ebook)

Printed in the United States of America

LSC-H

10 9 8 7 6 5 4 3 2 1

To all of my ancestors, especially my mother, Rachel,

for keeping the faith through the ages. And for my readers,

without whom this book would not have been written.

CONTENTS

CONTENTS

PART III.
SCRIPTURES

PART IV.
GOD AND COUNTRY

CONTENTS

GOD, FAITH,

and

REASON

Then said I: 'Ah, Lord GOD! behold,
I cannot speak; for I am a child.'

But the LORD said unto me:

Say not: I am a child;

For to whomsoever I shall send thee thou shalt go,

And whatsoever I shall command thee
thou shalt speak.

—Jeremiah 1:6–7

PREFACE

⁓

I never saw God, nor do I pretend to have any special insights. What you will see in this book are snapshots of God, not a complete film. This book is presented in an omnibus style and does not have to be read in precise, sequential order. What you will see is one man's glimpses of God—images along the road of life. I do not represent myself as a theologian or a guru. There are no cheap thrills here for the spiritually bankrupt masses. It is my scrapbook of the highest power through dreams, memories, and stories, much like the ancient texts.

My last book was a number one *New York Times* best seller, without any support from the media. It's my seventh book in a row that made the *New York Times* list, which is the gold standard of best-seller lists. Everyone reads it. So my publisher was thrilled. The people there said, "We want your next book."

But I said, "Hold on, now. I'm not doing another political book. I told my audience the last one would be my final political book." God gave me all my previous success. I knew my next book had to give something back to God.

My publisher agreed. They like me, and they figure that whatever I do, people will accept. I don't know if that's true. I don't know if my audience is ready for a book from me about the Bible and God. But I wrote it. I had to.

I know a lot of people who are not religious but say, "You know, it's terrible. We were once a great Christian nation, and the churches are empty and the mosques are filling up." They always want someone else to go to church. People who don't go to church don't really believe in God. They want someone to believe for them. They cry, "Oh, why are the churches empty?" To which I reply, "Well, why don't you go?" They aren't religious, but they wish other people were. Well, you are the other people.

Honour the LORD with thy substance,

And with the first-fruits of all thine increase;

So shall thy barns be filled with plenty,

And thy vats shall overflow with new wine.

—Proverbs 3:9–10

As I said many years ago, we've gone from St. Christopher medals to dream catchers in one generation. When I was a kid, it seemed as though every other car had a Catholic owner. They had little St. Christopher's statues on the dashboard. Myself, I didn't have one, but I liked that there were people who believed in God. And one day, I woke up, it was post-Obama and there were dream catchers hanging off mirrors. There are so many things hanging off mirrors, I don't know how people can see through their windshields. Mirrors and beads and voodoo. There is voodoo paraphernalia hanging off automobile mirrors and the country is melting down. It's total anarchy.

So what I'm trying to get at is that none of us lasts forever. There's an hourglass. You turn an hourglass upside down and you watch the sand trickle through. Well, in my case—and I'm not trying to pull a tearjerker on you—there's more sand on the bottom than there is on the top. There was a time when there was more sand on the top than on the bottom and I thought I had unlimited time to do everything. I don't. No one does.

What I'm saying to you is, I've just knocked another ball out of Yankee Stadium. It's called *Trump's War*. What more do I need to prove to myself or anyone else? I began as a writer. Fundamentally, that's what I am. But behind the writer, there's something else.

But this is very important for you to know: When I was down and out, I had to go down to the core of my being and reach out to the man upstairs, to put it colloquially. And I had to ask Him to save me.

It didn't happen like a boom went off or lightning struck or Charlton Heston appeared in my living room with a ticket to heaven. I had to keep asking for it. And it took me twenty years to climb out of that hole. See, God helps those who help themselves. He doesn't give you anything. By reaching out to God, maybe you can help yourselves.

I don't always practice what I preach. For example, I occasionally eat high-fat cheese, even though I've written health books. Once a year, I'll eat a hot dog. Twice a year, I'll eat a steak, even though I know it's poison for me. I know it. We all do things we know aren't good for us, but we do them anyway. It's the same spiritually, right?

Recently I was having bad dreams. I can sleep through them. I've learned how to live with that my whole life. It's nothing to me. I can sleep through the worst nightmare on Earth. I say to myself, "Oh, another one. That was great." I can't wait to go to sleep and see where my mind will take me tonight. What horror show awaits me?

I'd go to sleep, and it was like nightmare movies every night. I wouldn't wake up, though, because I learned a long time ago that it doesn't really matter if you have nightmares, if you sleep through them. It's like a bad movie. I thought, "Wait a minute, there must be a way for me to deal with this."

One day, I opened an ancient Hebrew prayer book that a very religious man had given me. There's a one-paragraph prayer that I've been reading for a while now. It's called "Prayer Before Retiring at Night." Is there magic? If religion doesn't work, it's of no use at all. If religion has no effect on your life, there's no reason to go to church or synagogue. In other words, if it doesn't make you feel better, what good is it? What, are you waiting for the next world? That's a big gamble, my friend. That's a huge gamble, to throw away all of life's pleasures on the chance that you're going to be rewarded in the next world. You begin to sound like those who think they're going to get seventy-two virgins, or whatever the number is, for killing you.

I can't live for the next world. I don't even know if there is a next world. This is the only earth I know of, and this earth is the only heaven that I know of. This is also the only hell I know of. But I figure that if this stuff has worked for others for thousands of years, there must be something to it. Are all those millions stupid? Are they all idiots?

And the word of the LORD came unto me, saying:

Before I formed thee in the belly I knew thee,

And before thou camest forth out of the
womb I sanctified thee;

I have appointed thee a prophet unto the nations.

— Jeremiah 1:4–5

And Joseph came in unto them in the morning, and saw them, and, behold, they were sad.

And he asked Pharaoh's officers that were with him in the ward of his master's house, saying: 'Wherefore look ye so sad to-day?'

And they said unto him: 'We have dreamed a dream, and there is none that can interpret it.'

And Joseph said unto them: 'Do not interpretations belong to God? tell it me, I pray you.'

— Genesis 40:6–8

Some people say they are. They say, "Religion is for idiots." Really? All those millions of people through history who were and are religious, they're all idiots? The ones criticizing them are the only smart ones?

I'm telling you all this because my dreams have stopped. At least the bad ones have. I sleep like a baby now. "Prayer Before Retiring at Night" is better than any herbal tea I've ever taken. Can I give you one paragraph? It begins, "Master of the Universe, I hereby forgive anyone who has angered or vexed me." That's the first thing you say. I say it, and the dog looks as though there's a different person in the room. He thinks I'm crazy. He sees me standing near the mirror with the book, and he's looking at me like, "What the heck are you doing now?"

"Master of the universe, I hereby forgive anyone who has angered or vexed me or sinned against me, either physically or financially, against my honor or anything else that is mine, whether accidentally or intentionally, inadvertently or deliberately, by speech or by deed, in this incarnation or in any other. May no man be punished on my account. May it be your will, Lord, my God, and God of my fathers, that I shall sin no more nor repeat my sins. Neither shall I again anger you nor do what is wrong in your eyes. The sins I have committed erase in your abounding mercies but not through suffering or severe illnesses."

They cover all bases there. "May the words of my mouth and the meditation of my heart be acceptable before you Lord, my strength and my redeemer. Our Father, let us lie down in peace. Our King, raise us up to do a good life and peace. Improve us . . ."

Do you see what I'm saying? In other words, you're supposed to forgive anyone who insulted you or robbed you or sinned against you in this life or any other. It allows you to go to sleep and not think about those things. Now, there's much more to this prayer before retiring at night, but I want to give you a little taste, in common parlance, of where my head is going. These are simple things that have calmed people for centuries and, in these anguishing times, it's very important to share with you some of these ancient methods of calming the human soul.

These are perplexing times. These are times that produce anxiety, and in our society, everyone has their own way of trying to deal with it: run, exercise, take a pill, drink tea, meditate, do Pilates, have sex . . . who knows? These are all things people use to calm themselves down. But the prayer I shared with you is a palliative that has been with us since the Rock of Ages was written. I wanted to share it with you because it's carried me through some very hard times. So, too, have many of the other experiences in the pages ahead.

This is not a "religious book." It's a quest and odyssey. You might ask why you should read someone else's odyssey. By the time you've finished this book, I hope you will have found the answer.

In this book, I will draw upon my personal experiences, the personal experiences of others, with God, without God; but most important, I will draw upon my personal copy of the five books of Moses the Jewish Bible. I have had this book for well over forty years. It has hundreds of little yellow Post-it notes that I have attached as I've read it for solace. My hope is to do service to God who created all of us.

But from thence ye will seek the LORD thy God;

and thou shalt find Him, if thou search after Him

with all thy heart and with all thy soul.

—Deuteronomy 4:29

PART I.

DOES GOD EXIST?

$\mathfrak{I}$n the beginning God created the heaven
and the earth.

Now the earth was unformed and void, and darkness
was upon the face of the deep; and the spirit of God
hovered over the face of the waters.

— Genesis 1:1–2

Does God exist?

What is the nature of God?

What is the nature of man?

There are people far more knowledgeable than I regarding the Bible, the Hebrew, the meaning, the theology, etc. But it does not mean they know anything more about God than you or I do. You can take the most ordinary person who is a believer, and I've met them, and they do more for inspiring the nonbeliever than does the most intelligent, intellectual theologian on the planet. God is about belief and faith. It is not about proving there is a God, for there is no proof. What proof can there be?

If there were a firm proof, there would be no need for this book. It would've been done a thousand times by now. The fact that we're even contemplating whether God exists indicates that nobody really knows. But I say the obverse tells us that God does exist.

For example, you run into a person who says, "I'm an atheist. I don't believe God exists." What does that do for the universe? Does God cease to exist because one person out of the billions who are living and the billions who have lived suddenly says, "God doesn't exist"? Is that person so narcissistic as to believe that because he or she says, "I don't believe in God," that, therefore, God doesn't exist? That's absurd. God doesn't need that individual to prove His existence.

No, my friends, the fact of the matter was stated to me by a hobo I met many years ago in the streets of San Francisco. As we spoke, and I looked into his startlingly blue eyes with a shock of white hair, I asked him (he told me his name was Moses), "Moses, do you believe in God?" He looked at me in a puzzled manner and replied, "Who do you think created me?" That solved it for me. I have met many believing people who don't need proof. That's what I'm trying to say to you. This is not a book that will try to prove to you that God exists. Not at all. God doesn't need Michael Savage to prove His existence. Michael Savage needs to write this book to prove to himself that Michael Savage exists.

Does God exist? This question has plagued mankind from the beginning of recorded history. Even the saintly Mother Teresa admitted in her last years that, many times in her life, she did not know the answer to this question. Yet we live as if God does exist and as if there will be a Judgment Day when we will be judged for our good and bad deeds. But what is good and what is bad? That has become increasingly confusing in this age of relativity. There seem to be no mores that are considered universal. Can that be so?

Look at the Ten Commandments. Read all of them. "Thou shall not kill." What does that mean? Aren't we told to kill in war? Well, if you read the original Hebrew, the word is "murder." The commandment is "Thou shall not murder." It does not say, "Thou shall not kill." They are two completely different things. It takes some knowledge of the history of both the Hebrew language and of the prophets themselves to properly interpret not only the Ten Commandments but mankind's guidebook for life on this earth, the Bible.

As I take you on this journey with me, I ask you to have patience, for I am neither a prophet nor a holy man. I am just a man who has thought about the questions we will explore together in the pages that follow since the beginning of my consciousness. Why was I put here? Why were you put here? Why are we born if we're born to die? Why must we suffer? Why does God forsake even the good among us? Why do little children suffer so terribly in cancer wards around the world? Why are so many good men and women slaughtered in war? Why do evil men thrive, unpunished in their lifetimes?

Many of you have given up on God. You think it's nonsense. You haven't been in a church or a synagogue your entire adult life. Some of you are Jewish. You had a bar mitzvah and that was the last time you were in a temple. Oh, once in a while, you observe Rosh Hashanah. You do the mumbo jumbo; you put on the hat. And then you go and have a meal and think you did your thing. Or you come back to do a thing for the dead.

You tell yourself you don't really believe in it, but there's a little tiny part of you that does. And what will happen is, as you get older, it will become bigger and bigger and bigger. When you're young, you can believe in nothing except your pleasure center. That's the norm. That's the way it's supposed to be. But as you get older, as things happen to you, as things break in your body, you want to turn to somebody. But you don't know where to turn. These questions have plagued me to such an extent that I have lost my faith many times along the rocky road we all walk. But we all must walk along this road, no matter how much our feet bleed, no matter how they ache.

Years ago, I stumbled upon a small book entitled *Peace of Mind*. In it, the author wrote that he does not believe that God is omnipotent. He is omnipresent, meaning He is everywhere at all times, but He does not control everything that occurs. He wrote that if he believed that God was omnipotent and controlled everything that happens—babies with cancer, innocent men and women slaughtered, innocent children raped—he would cease to believe and become an atheist on the spot.

But he concluded that God is in fact not omnipotent but only omnipresent, meaning we do have free will and control our destinies. Yes, there are things encoded in us, perhaps through genetics, perhaps through faith, that we cannot control. Perhaps we are born for certain faiths. But within the parameters of these genetic or predetermined destinies, we have wide latitude. And that is why we need the guidebook called the Holy Bible.

Fear thou not, for I am with thee,

Be not dismayed, for I am thy God;

I strengthen thee, yea, I help thee;

Yea, I uphold thee with My victorious right hand.

—Isaiah 41:10

Faith and Reason

Now, why would I throw the word *reason* in when faith is the opposite of reason? If you're an educated person who also believes in God, there is almost a dichotomy there. People call my show, *The Savage Nation*, and ask, "How can you believe in God and be a rational man? How can a rational man believe in a figment of the imagination, some kind of voodoo that was created to hoodwink people thousands of years ago in ancient Palestine?"

Judaism was the progenitor of the three major religions, the other two being Christianity and Islam. Many people may not know that it was Judaism first, then Christianity, then Islam. So the three Abrahamic religions, the three monotheistic religions, go back to Judaism.

Many people still ask, "How do you know?" They argue that people were so wild in those days in Israel, those ancient olive growers, there had to be controls. So they came up with some myth about Heaven and a burning bush to scare them that if they didn't do the right thing, they'd be punished in the next world. How can a rational person believe in God?

Well, I'm a very rational person, as evidenced by many things I've achieved. I think logically, up to a point. But faith is something

And your sons and your daughters shall prophesy,

Your old men shall dream dreams,

Your young men shall see visions;

— Joel 3:1

different from reason, isn't it? That's why the title of this book is *God, Faith, and Reason.* I do not believe that reason is incompatible with faith. Faith is believing in something, whether it's reasonable or not.

I believe in God. I'm a superrational man, up to a point. But I'm also a believer. The mystical Jews say the actual writings about God are in the white spaces between the letters. That's a conundrum unto itself. Well, it's the blank spaces in talk radio that explain who the host is. What you *don't* hear in between what you *do* hear is what you *should* hear.

I have often thought about arguments concerning reason and religion. Are reason and religion compatible? I need to hear them from an educated person who believes in God. In other words, I'm not knocking you if you didn't have the chance to go to college and get a higher degree and become a doctor or lawyer or engineer, but I often wonder about engineers who are rationalists and also believe in God, because if you're an engineer you are an utter rationalist. How do you make that compatible? How does that work?

The photographer who took the cover pic for *Teddy and Me* also took the picture for the cover of this book. The session didn't go well at first. I don't like posing for pictures. I don't like to do television. I'm a terrible author for my publisher's marketing department. I don't like to be seen; I like to be heard.

I said to him, "Look, I'm not a hero. I'm simply a writer and a broadcaster. What you see is what you get. If you want a heroic pose, you'll have to hire an actor." But just before he left, he tried one more time to get what he wanted. It was drizzling outside, and I was sitting on the edge of a sofa with rain falling behind me. And he caught something in my eyes that reveals a different Michael Savage. Maybe it was another part of me. Maybe it was the real me, the essence of me. I'm not sure, but it's the Michael Savage I want you to see. I'm not trying to convert you to religion or sell you on religion. I just want you to feel what I've seen in these snapshots of God.

I don't know of a man or woman on earth, not even an atheist or communist, who hasn't explored this question. I would say that even the leftists who listen to my show purely to mock me afterward have at some point in their lives thought about God. It amazes me that people won't even talk about it anymore. They're afraid or ashamed to show their vulnerability to this higher power. They don't want to reveal that they are not all-powerful themselves.

Everyone wants to act like a macho person who controls everything. I think that's the basis of it all, the narcissism, the ego, the vanity. Who was it who said, "All is vanity"?

Are faith and reason incompatible? I know some highly educated people who are very religious. And I know scoffers who say, "How can you, as an educated man, believe in God?"

Reason leads to faith. In fact, the greater your reasoning powers, the purer your reasoning powers, the greater your mathematical abilities, ultimately they will lead to an understanding of God.

I will cite one example. Albert Einstein said the further he got out into the thought process of the universe, the more he realized

The whole head is sick,

And the whole heart faint;

—Isaiah 1:5

there had to be a greater power that had created it all. There was no other explanation. You'll find that the higher your own reasoning power becomes, the more you'll realize that reason doesn't answer every question. Instead, it leads you to faith. If it doesn't lead you to faith, you'll really be in trouble. It will lead you to drugs and rehab and the destruction of your soul.

To me, reason and faith are twins. They aren't identical twins; they're fraternal twins.

One day, I asked my producer to lead into a show segment with the song "I Believe." The lyrics are astounding:

Every time I hear a newborn baby cry,
Or touch a leaf, or see the sky,
Then I know why I believe.

For fathers reading this book, think back to when your first child was born. Think about what it was like to be in that delivery room when your child came into this world. I have spoken to men who have told me it changed their lives forever. That's when a man becomes a different person. He may have been a tough guy before, but he's a different man afterward. When he sees the head of his daughter or his son enter this world, he changes forever.

You can't talk about it. There are no words for this. There is no painting for it. All the sonograms in the world don't do for you what that does for you. That's why I recommend that all men be present when their children are born. It will make you a different man, forever. It won't perfect you in any way. You'll probably be the same person, but you'll be a different same person.

I devoted most of an entire episode of *The Savage Nation* to the question of whether faith and reason are compatible. I put the question to my listeners and invited them to call in with their

thoughts on the matter. Some of their insights were quite remark-
able. One was particularly interesting to me.

It was a man whose wife was very sick. She was really suffering
and in a lot of pain. Her doctors, "in their infinite wisdom," as he
put it, took her pain medication away. The poor woman screamed
for two straight days. It got so bad she actually told the man she
wanted to die.

As you can probably imagine, that put a lot of pressure on
him, too. He became so desperate himself that he prayed, "God,
please take me out of here. I can't bear to hear this, not one second
more. I can't take it."

God answered his prayer, although not the way he expected
Him to. The man said he suddenly felt like he was hurtling down-
ward, even though he was still on the couch with his wife. The
world as he knew it seemed to disappear as he descended.

Then he found himself standing in a very dark place. But he
wasn't alone. He could feel the presence of several entities next to
him. And somehow he knew those beings were vile and meant
him harm. They spoke to him, telling him what they were going
to do to him, and he said their words seemed to go right through
him. And although his story sounded like a nightmare, he said he
could also feel how very real what was happening was and how
real that place was.

There was only one thing he could say at that moment. "Please,
God, save me," he prayed. As soon as he spoke those words, it
was apparent that the beings speaking to him could not bear to
hear God's name. Immediately, he had the sensation of ascending. He was now rising out of that dark place even faster than he
had fallen into it. All the while, he was still on the same couch he
had sat on with his wife, now ascending at dizzying speed. Finally
his spirit rejoined his body. He described the sensation as being

like "sticking a finger into an outlet with no pain." Then he heard a voice speaking to him that said, "I've given you what you asked for."

Just then his wife looked at him and said she felt very tired and wanted to go to sleep. And she slept for ten straight hours without any pain medicine, a more peaceful rest than she'd had in months.

The man said the experience had taught him about how much power lies within each human being. "You have the power to give up your spirit," he said, "to give up the right that you have to live." But ultimately God will save you if you ask him to. When the man was literally in Hell, being threatened by demons, God did not leave him there for a moment after he asked for God's help. There was no Purgatory for him. God did not remind him of all the sins he had committed and make him suffer in the darkness to atone for them. The moment he asked for salvation, he was saved.

No shrub of the field was yet in the earth,
And no herb of the field had yet sprung up;

— Genesis 2:5

What a call that was. The caller said he had seen Hell. Now, if you're not living in a place called Hell, if you're not suffering at the moment, that's great. But that's not going to be the way it is all the way to the end. I don't care if you're the coolest rap star on Earth, Mr. Cool, you're made of the same flesh and bone as we are.

Get back to me when you're seventy-eight and in the throes of cancer, if you get that far, and let me know what you believe in then. I guarantee you'll come back to your grandmother's faith at that point. You'll hear your grandmother sing to you when you're in that cancer ward, I can guarantee it as I'm standing here. You'll see the strongest man break down and cry and beg for his mother when he's in pain. I've seen that, too.

You'll see it all, believe me, if you haven't seen it already, because the mind is a kaleidoscope. Go back to the old Beatles song about me being you, and you being me, and we being all together. There is a lot of truth in some of those psychedelic songs.

I had another caller who was a biology professor, a man of science. He had this to say: "Dr. Savage, I'm a biology professor with six earned degrees. I've written a book about God and science, and I believe that history, logic, and philosophy actually lead to a belief in God. So I think that faith is reasonable and that faith is rational."

"Hold on," I said. "I want to take your first statement and go with it. You're saying sort of what I said, in your own way, which is that ultimately logic leads us to faith. Isn't that what you're saying?"

"Yes, I think so," he replied. "I think it's something that's discoverable by faith and there are a lot of good, logical, philosophical arguments that make belief in God a reasonable thing and a rational thing."

I myself go back and forth between a fervent belief that God exists and not believing there is anything out there. I'm not alone in that. It was a great day for me when I read about Mother Teresa's own struggles with this question. What a selfless woman she was, working with the sick, and not just in a soup kitchen on Thanksgiving like the liberals of San Francisco dishing out mashed potatoes and then holding their noses as they run away, to make believe how good they are. Mother Teresa worked with the poor and the sick every day.

But in her last days, her journals were published, and in them she said there were many days she had completely lost faith in the idea that God exists. And other days, she'd get it back. That's a real human being.

Mother Teresa also inspired another caller on my show, who started out answering my question about faith and reason but then brought up a separate but related question not about belief in God, per se, but belief in eternal life. We had the following interesting exchange. It began with his answer to my question on faith and reason.

"I'm a math major and also a believer in God and I like the title of your book, *God, Faith, and Reason*, because I believe faith serves as a bridge between the gap of man's finite ability to reason and God's infinite ability to do so."

I replied, "The skeptics are going to say, 'What's the reason for God giving cancer to children?'"

He answered, "I think there's three things at play, Dr. Savage. There is God's will, free will, and evil. And I don't think it's God's will for things like that to happen. I think it's free will and evil that take a role when God merely allows things like that to happen."

I said, "In other words, He doesn't control everything that happens everywhere at all times."

"Right," he said. "You make mention of the Old Testament. You look at the Book of Job, and God allows Satan to take away everything Job had achieved."

"That's what we all fear," I told him. "We all fear that with one mistake in our later years, everything will be wiped away from us.

The Jewish writers, the old-timers, would write that a man could spend his entire life creating his reputation, and with one mistake he could destroy his entire life. So we walk on these hot coals right to the end, don't we?"

"Yes," replied my caller, "but there's also knowing, and that's where faith kicks in, about eternal life."

I told him, "I don't know about eternal life. I don't profess to have seen any proof of it. But I've been seeking evidence of God my whole life, wherever I've gone. In all the years I was alone in the islands, picking plants, whether it was Fiji, Taga, Samoa, the Marquesas, in the most remote places on Earth, in every plant I picked, in every leaf I picked, in every medicinal plant I studied, I basically saw confirmation that God exists.

"If I was obsessed as I was for fifteen years, maybe longer, with finding healing properties in plants, what was I really trying to confirm? That God created these plants with these healing properties. This was God's medicine right there."

"Right," he said. "And you mentioned Mother Teresa. I cannot believe, with all the good that she did on this earth, that she is not in a better place and having eternal life."

Glimpses in Literature

I remember when I was a teenager and didn't know who I was; I remember very well the sufferings of being young. The adolescent years are very hard for all of us. They form us in many ways. I was an ordinary kid in so many ways and am today an ordinary man in many ways. But I remember, as a teenager, I would go to dances like everyone else, race cars illegally on Sunrise Highway like everyone else. I'd get grease on my hands like everyone else; I'd get into car wrecks like everyone else. I'd chase girls like everyone else.

But I wasn't *like* everyone else. I was uniquely myself. And when I got into that corner of trying to understand it all, I would turn to reading. I read a lot of Jack Kerouac, which may surprise you. But he led me to some great places. I read Henry Miller. You may say, "Oh, Henry Miller is a sex writer." No, he wasn't. He wrote about sex, but all his writings about sex were really leading to questions about existence.

I read those books from cover to cover, and I found some things in them that saved me. I remember reading *Black Spring* during one of my black springs. I was living through a black spring because of the social engineers attempting to deprive me of my birthright in this country. They deprived me of my right to make a living to give people who were less qualified than me positions I should have been offered. They passed me by because I was a white male.

I had to go to literature to survive. It was through literature such as *Black Spring* that I came to a deeper understanding of my place and time and allowed me to come to where I am today and to achieve what I've achieved today.

Hopefully, it will continue to allow me to go forward. I have a few plays left in me.

What I came to understand while taking some time off from my show is that when you're as immersed in radio and writing as I am, almost to the point of exhaustion, it takes something out of you. And then when you have that blank time, when you have nothing to do, you realize what it took out of you.

It's easy to get caught up in the fervor of work, work, work, until you don't even know what you're doing and how hard you're working. And then when you get four days off, as I did, a bottom falls out of you. You'd better have a place to land.

Luckily, I landed where I started when I was a teenager, which was reading literature. That has given me the understanding in my meditation on where I'm at, which is having a few plays left in me. You may be very surprised when you hear what's coming in my professional life in the coming months.

It's a rebirth. I'm like a born-again Savage. Some huge things are in my future, but I wasn't even sure I wanted to do them. But now I know I want to do them because God wants me to do them. I have a mission to save America. That's why I've worked for almost a quarter century to awaken America, before we lose America.

And the child grew, and was weaned.

And Abraham made a great feast on the day

that Isaac was weaned.

— Genesis 21:8

Indignation

While writing this book, I had a rare four consecutive days off from *The Savage Nation*. And just by chance, I caught the movie *Indignation*, based on the novel of the same name by Philip Roth. It's about a guy who goes to college in the 1950s, coming from a background very like mine. His father was a butcher; he worked in the butcher shop with him. My father was an antiques dealer; I worked with him. The main character is a very dutiful son. He gets straight A's.

I couldn't believe they were showing that movie while I was writing this book. The movie wasn't that good; it lacked all the great elements of the book. But I'd read the book, and the movie reminded me about how relevant it is to the book you are reading, believe it or not.

Philip Roth is one of the great American novelists, a true gift to humanity. Sadly, many people in our time don't even know who he is anymore. He is very satisfying to read because of the depth of his stories, even though they're usually based on a sexual theme. But he takes the sexual theme and turns it into something much deeper. Sex doesn't have to be shallow.

In the novel, the main character wants to leave his father to go to college. His father is oppressing him. Plus, the Korean War is raging and the protagonist believes that if he doesn't get straight A's and get into college, he will be drafted, sent to Korea, and killed.

So he applies to a small Midwestern college to get away from the butcher, who is driving him crazy. His father isn't driving him crazy just to hurt him. Rather, his father is mad with fear and apprehension of the dangers of adult life, the dangers of the war, the danger he sees everywhere, in every corner, for his beloved son. And he doesn't leave his boy alone.

The boy wants to be free. He doesn't realize his father's fear arises from love and pride. But it produces so much anger in the boy that he leaves his father and gets as far away from Newark as he can. And he must adopt the customs and culture of another American world, the Midwest.

In the book, the nineteen-year-old protagonist has a relationship, if you want to call it that, with a beautiful young girl he meets in the library. The girl performs a certain sexual act upon him the first night, in the car. And he's freaked out. He doesn't understand it. He thinks she's a slut. And then he sees she has a scar on her hand, that she's a cutter. She cuts herself.

Later in the book, the reader finds out that the protagonist is dead. He has been drafted, sent to the Korean War, and killed. And he is speaking from the grave. That was so daring for Roth to do. That is the difference between literature and the dreck most people consume, pulp fiction.

But the protagonist has a series of arguments with the dean of the college, who doesn't understand this kid because he's a rebel. The kid can't get along with any of the roommates they put him in with. He moves out twice. They think he's a malcontent. He can't fit in.

At that college, in those days, you had to go to chapel forty times a year to graduate. The protagonist doesn't want to do this. He's a lover of Bertrand Russell, who wrote "Why I Am Not a Christian." Russell, a total rationalist, is one of the protagonist's heroes. The boy is an atheist, doesn't believe in a higher power. The dean doesn't understand how he can get through life without believing.

In one of the protagonist's arguments with the dean, who is trying to understand him or at least get him under control, he says to the dean about Bertrand Russell:

> He says, "If everything must have a cause, then God must have a cause. If there can be anything without a cause, it may just as well be the world as God." Second, as to the argument from design, he says, "Do you think that, if you were granted omnipotence and omniscience and millions of years in which to perfect your world, you could produce nothing better than the Ku Klux Klan or the Fascists?"

The young student goes on to regurgitate Russell's critiques of Christ and his teaching, along with Russell's doubts about Christ's very existence. Russell condemned Jesus Christ for believing in Hell, calling it inhumane, and blamed the Church for retarding human progress. He said that religion is based primarily on fear of anything unknown, including defeat and death. And because fear begets cruelty, he says, religion and cruelty have "gone hand in hand" throughout history.

The young man is especially enamored by Russell's association of atheism with freedom. Russell believes that pure reason or intelligence should govern one's life but that fear of the unknown, of life itself, keeps men "slavishly subdued." So belief in God is a manifestation of man's fear, "unworthy of free men." The student arrogantly tells the dean, "These are the thoughts of a Nobel Prize winner, renowned for his contributions to philosophy and for his mastery of logic and the theory of knowledge, and I find myself in total agreement with them." He goes on to say that he not only agrees with and intends to live by Bertrand Russell's principles but believes it is his *right* to do so. You can see the seeds of today's politically correct campuses, where any mention of God is banned.

The dean counters him. Of course, it's the writer taking the dean's side in the argument. He tells the young man that he admires his spirit, confidence, and tenacity and believes the young man will be an outstanding lawyer. "I can see you one day arguing a case before the Supreme Court of the United States. And winning it, young man, winning it," he tells him.

But for all his admiration of the student's intelligence and ability to internalize Russell's arguments, he is dismayed by the young man's willingness to accept those arguments without question. This is a great insight into the revolutionary ethos, especially insofar as it is found in the minds of the young. The college campus rebel bravely questions the existence of God or long-standing societal customs but never thinks to question that which he seeks to replace them with. The dean takes the young student to task for precisely this:

> "I admire your ability to memorize and retain abstruse reading matter even if I don't necessarily admire whom and what you choose to read and the gullibility with which you take at face value rationalist blasphemies spouted by an immoralist of the ilk of Bertrand Russell, four times married, a blatant adulterer, an advocate of free love, a self-confessed socialist, dismissed from his university position for his antiwar campaigning during the First War and imprisoned for that by the British authorities."

"What about the Nobel Prize!" demands the student, hammering his fist on the desk and pointing his finger at the dean.

The dean again commends the student for his fighting spirit, adding that he wishes the student were moved to such passion for a worthier cause than Bertrand Russell, whom the dean obviously believes the British government was justified in labeling a subversive. But then the dean makes one of the more insightful comments in the book:

> "To find that Bertrand Russell is a hero of yours comes as no great surprise. There are always one or two intellectually precocious youngsters on every campus, self-appointed members of an elite intelligentsia who need to elevate themselves and feel superior to their fellow students, superior even to their professors, and so pass through the phase of finding an agitator or iconoclast to admire on the order of a Russell or a Nietzsche or a Schopenhauer. Nonetheless, these views are not what we are here to discuss, and it is certainly your prerogative to admire whomever you like, however deleterious the influence and however dangerous the consequences of such a so-called freethinker and self-styled reformer may seem to me."

As I read that, I said to myself, "My God, is he ever describing the attitude of the pseudo-intellectuals on television and in other media. They truly are 'intellectually precocious youngsters.'" That would be especially a person like Macho Madcow, who is like a precocious college kid, with that sneering face, always sneering to her girlfriends in the sorority, to show how she's superior to the average person out there.

So when you think about "elitists," think about them as not so elite after all. They're not so elite. They've ruined the world, not only in the media but in everything they've touched.

Reading this dialogue did something good for me. It made me think very hard about this book and revise my thinking about it, as literature has done in my life before. When you associate your mind with greats, your mind improves, your mind goes to new places. As the Jewish Kabbalists said, it's the white between the letters, not the black ink you see, that is important. That's something very hard to comprehend unless you've thought about mysticism.

But it's the spaces and the breaths I've taken, between what I've said on the air, that carry the meaning of what I've tried to say. I can't explain it. I wish I could.

Without trying to be too clever or too tricky, let me explain what happened to me when I read *Indignation* again. It brought me back to a new place that I had lost. I had wandered away from my own depth. It has a lot to do with the radio business and what's gone on in talk radio. It has evolved to a point where I almost couldn't take another day of it. I was reaching a point where I couldn't do one more day of that trite garbage.

If I had to listen to one more day of people bashing liberals, as if it were something brand new that no one had ever said before, every day the same thing, "Democrat bad, Republican good," I don't know if I could have gone on. I'd rather retire and spend the rest of my life reading novels and taking care of dogs and elephants and whales and giving money to animal causes. I didn't even want to talk. I wanted to take a vow of silence. I didn't want to live in that polluted stream of triteness. I couldn't take it.

But after rereading the novel, I felt like I could go back to my audience and bring them something worthy of their *ear time*. I could feel that my connection with my audience was back. I could feel it, and I know the audience could feel it. The old Savage was back.

So man lieth down and riseth not;

Till the heavens be no more, they shall not awake,

Nor be roused out of their sleep.

— Job 14:12

Dinner with an Atheist
and a Buddhist

I recently had dinner with a psychiatrist who is a stone-hearted atheist. He has told me on several walks together that he doesn't believe in the hereafter and doesn't believe in God. He believes that when the electrical energy in the brain stops, that's it. It's over.

Interestingly, he asked me at dinner when this book was coming out. I told him it would be out just in time for this year's holidays. I learned for the first time that as a child he had been taken to church every day by his very religious mother, which I found to be very interesting.

Also at the table was an Asian friend of mine, who disclosed to me his Buddhist belief system. Unto itself, that's not such a great revelation, but what follows is. I asked him and his wife if they believe in a hereafter, if they believe in reincarnation. He said he does believe in reincarnation and went on to explain the following.

He told us that his own mother says his wife being married to him is her penance for a past life sin against him in another form, in another place.

I said, "What? Say that again?"

He said, "Oh yes, my mother says that my beautiful wife has put up with me all these twenty-some odd years as part of her penance for a sin she committed against me in another life."

I started to laugh and said, "I didn't know Buddhist mothers were more condemning of their sons than Jewish mothers," which is quite funny in its own way. I continued, "How does that work?"

His wife then said, "In the next life, we may come back where I'm the husband and he's the wife. Or he could be my son, I could be his mother."

In other words, from the Buddhist point of view, it's a way of balancing everything out through time. I don't know if this makes sense to a non-Buddhist, but Buddhists believe that everything is balanced through time and reincarnation. I thought that was a great insight into Buddhism. I had never heard it explained in that way.

As for the atheist doctor, I'm still not sure if he really believes that life is finite and ends when the electrical energy in the brain ends, having learned that he went to church with his mother every day.

I ran this whole story by a friend of mine, who interpreted it in an opposite way. My friend said that the Buddhist man's mother was not putting her son down by saying, "Whatever you do to her or have done for twenty years is payback for what she did to you in a past life." My friend said she interprets that to mean that the wife so hurt him in another life that whatever he does to her is okay. So the mother was actually justifying his behavior toward his wife. It's her fault! What he meant by, "has put up with me," whether it was gambling, running with other women, or God knows what, it's her fault. In other words, it's okay to do it.

It's Impossible to Prove That God Does Not Exist

Why does God do this to us? It's not a question of proving that God exists. All I can think is that it's impossible that He doesn't exist. It's as though my mind has reached the point of saying it can't all be an accident. It can't be. It's impossible.

There's no possibility that we're a *National Geographic* creation run by a bunch of crazed leftists, anyway. Almost every show on the National Geographic Channel seems to try to show that God doesn't exist, that there was a speck of dust in the universe, then carbon fell down and mixed up with the oxygen in the swamp and the slime, and other molecules, and here we are trying on clothing in department stores. It doesn't make sense to me.

No matter where my mind goes on a scientific level, I am a total believer. What does that do for you? Nothing. What does it mean for me? Everything. Because I'm confident that this is the way it's supposed to be, even when bad things happen. Let's go into bad things.

I've had minor bad things happen to me, not major ones. Major bad things include losing a child, God forbid; getting cancer; having a heart attack; not being able to talk; having a stroke; or developing Alzheimer's disease. Those are bad, bad things. Going broke after you have a little money is another. One of the most devastating things that could happen to you is to have some success, lose it all, and wind up back where you started or worse. That's probably one of the worst things that could happen.

What is God's plan? I don't know. How do you deal with bad, bad things? How do you deal with a child dying of leukemia in a cancer ward? What are you going to say? It was his karma? He was a bad person in another life? I don't want to accept that.

That's why the book *Peace of Mind* stayed with me. If God is omnipresent but not omnipotent, He does not control every aspect of our lives. He doesn't control our every breath. We have free will in that regard.

In other words, God starts the clock and then the clock runs. You are the clock. Where you go with what you are given is another story.

⟡

And ye shall seek Me, and find Me, when ye
shall search for Me with all your heart.

—Jeremiah 29:13

⟡

Papers in the Street

I have in my hand a well-worn, brown, almost worn-out little business card from my father that I recently received from a family member. It has his name and antiques store address, 137 Ludlow Street, New York 2, New York. And on the back of it is my grandfather's name, the petition number from his citizen papers, which say Russia and Poland, and also the names of the three children he brought with him.

Apparently, my father made notes on the card for his immigrant father, who I assume couldn't write for himself. I look at the card, and I wonder what their struggles must have been. My grandfather Sam was the astronaut of the family, having left behind the old world and come here without his family, eventually bringing over his wife and then his three children. He died of a heart attack very young at age forty-seven, no doubt from struggle, worry, and cigarettes. God knows what.

I mention his card in this book because I wonder how much God played a role in Sam's life. As far as I know, I do not come from a religious family at all. My father, Benjamin, was an atheist who didn't believe in a greater being. He was very cynical about religion.

The opening of Thy words giveth light;

It giveth understanding unto the simple.

I opened wide my mouth, and panted;

For I longed for Thy commandments.

— Psalms 119:130–31

As for me, religion entered my life strangely. Actually, I don't think it entered. I think it was always there. I have one memory. I was a young boy, maybe five years old, running in the streets of the Bronx. And I remember a Jewish newspaper was blowing in the wind. I didn't understand a word of it, but because it was written in another language that I thought was a holy language, I assumed it was holy writing, I picked up every sheet of it, took them home, and said to my mother, "Look what I found in the street. I saved it," thinking I had saved some holy text. Well, it obviously was just a newspaper written in either Hebrew or Yiddish, but I didn't know that. There are other distant memories of my relationship to my ancestral language and my ancestral religion, which will come up throughout this book.

— ∞◦◦◦ —

And God created man in His own image,

in the image of God created He him;

male and female created He them.

— Genesis 1:27

— ∞◦◦◦ —

A Four-Year-Old's
View of God

My friend, Daniel, has two lovely children. His little daughter, Chloe, is four years old. He said that she wanted to learn about Hanukkah, so he bought her a book on it for Christmas. She asked him to read it to her. He got to the part where the Greeks took over the temple, and she asked, "Daddy, what is a temple?"

Daniel said, "It was a Jewish White House." In those days, religion and politics were the same.

Then the questions from that precocious four-year-old resumed. She asked, "Why does God want us to have a temple?"

He said, "I don't know, but that is where people go to talk to God."

She asked, "What do they say to Him?"

"Well, they say a lot of things. They thank God for making everything."

She asked, "Why did He make everything?"

He said, "I don't know, but we are here and we're trying to explain why."

"Well, what did He make us out of?"

Dan said, "Well, people believe that God made us from nothing."

She asked, "But why did He do it?"

"There are many views on that."

"Who made Him?"

"Well, that's the big question," he said. "If there was nothing, then who made God? A bigger God? Also, if God could do anything, can He make a car that everyone else can drive but He can't?"

She said, "I know, Daddy, it doesn't make sense. What do you think?"

He told her, "I think that you will have to decide for yourself and pick answers that are best for you."

He then showed her the Ten Commandments, which are in the book, and he told her, "Here's the good part. Honor your mother and father." The little girl smiled.

Then he read the part that said, "Thou shalt not murder." Chloe said, "But you can protect yourself."

He said, "Yes. Just not murder someone. Murder is killing without defending someone."

"Murder is killing without defending someone?" she asked. "But people are doing that already." She then asked, "How do we know that God really gave us the Ten Commandments? How do we know this?"

He said, "It's what people believe based upon what is in the book." Dan then tried to put Judaism together with his wife, Val's, Episcopalian background, and he said, "The Ten Commandments is a part of both of our religions. It is God's instructions to the Jews."

The child asked, "But what about Jesus, Daddy? Was he God?"

He said, "The Jews see him as a Jew. He followed Jewish law, and he was really, really smart. If he was God as a person, or a Jew who was really smart and kind, it doesn't matter. Both are good."

Therefore the Lord Himself shall give you a sign:
behold, the young woman shall conceive, and bear a son,
and shall call his name Immanuel.

—Isaiah 7:14

"But, Dad, why would God be a person? What does God really look like?"

Dan said, "I think God can be a boy or girl or anything God wants."

"Well, how was he born if he was God?"

Dan said, "He was born as a Jew. That is for sure. The Christians believe that wise people knew of his birth and he was very special right from the beginning. So we both agree that he was special, but the Christians believe he was special because he was God on Earth."

Chloe asked, "But why would God want people to see a baby born? How did they know to come to see him?"

Daniel said, "I don't know. That's what they believe: that somehow they knew."

Chloe said, "That doesn't make sense to me. Why would God want people to visit a baby? I want to see this in a book. Did anyone write about this?"

You can see where this is going. The fact of the matter is that children are more rational than adults in many ways, and they want strictly rational answers to questions for which there are no answers. That's what makes them so insightful. This is the essence of faith. Faith is the ability of a human being to believe in something for which there is no proof.

Fundamentally, that's the whole point of this book: to believe in God, you must have faith. There is no proof that God exists.

Is God Real?

S ometimes I ask myself, "What is real?" We're living in a society where everything is fake. The food is fake. Nothing tastes good anymore. Ersatz wine is chemicalized, as are the air, the water, everything. And, of course, we all know the news is fake. Were the media ever the harbingers of truth? No, they always made up what they were feeding us, by and large, with a few notable exceptions. We have too much fake science. For example, inventing whole phony disciplines to support the climate change hoax, which is a political movement, not a scientific one.

What do you turn to, my dear, beloved readers? Where do you turn when you want something real? Every institution we grew up with in this country has been blown up. There is almost nothing left. And I'm not talking about older people. Not at all. I think they still have their religion, their family, and their values. But society at large is a different story.

How can everyone else decide who and what is real? How can you judge who is real? How can you know if a person you are talking to, a person you get to know, a person you do business with, or a person you are dating is real?

I asked some of my listeners on *The Savage Nation* these same questions. Here is what one of them had to say:

"I would like to say that for an inward reflection in realness, hobbies. Personal hobbies, like playing an instrument, knowing exactly what's in it, as far as, there's not going to be any autotune," said one caller.

"Exactly," I replied. "And you're either good at it, poor at it, or mediocre at it. You know it, and so does everyone around you. So playing music is real."

Cooking was another great example that came out of that call. There is no way to fake cooking, even if the food is fake. Either it comes out tasting good or it doesn't.

These are the basics that keep people going in a time where everything around them seems fraudulent. I find myself most at rest when I'm doing something with my hands, when I'm making or fixing something. That's when I feel most stable. Gardening is one example. Seeing my peaches ripen and my tomatoes come up is real to me. I know I probably sound like the character in *The Godfather* in the garden, waiting to fall over. But there is something so real about planting tiny tomato plants and seeing them produce tomatoes three months later. That's real.

There is a divinity in growing vegetables, which may explain why so many primitive cultures centered their religious beliefs around it. That and necessity, of course. Women enjoy an especially direct connection to producing life by bearing children.

My mind wanders when I talk to people. I don't consider it a shortcoming. Some people can't listen to other people. First, I do it every day on the radio. So when I get off the air, I don't really want to listen to anybody. It can be hard to be around me for that reason. People can see my eyes rolling after thirty seconds, or they can see I'm stressing to make believe I'm listening.

Do you think I don't know this? I know who I am and what I am. I live with it. There's an oft-used phrase, "Comfortable in your own skin." I'm pretty comfortable in mine. Do I have a choice? After all these years, I don't know how to be uncomfortable in my own body. We've lived together for so long. We certainly can't separate and become a duality. At least not in this life. Tomorrow it could all be over. But for the grace of God, right?

Here's a typical morning prayer some religious Jews read to start the day:

> Blessed are you, Lord our God, King of the universe, Who has formed man in wisdom, and created within him numerous orifices and cavities. It is revealed and known before the Throne of Your Glory that if but one of them were to be blocked, or one of them were to be opened, it would be impossible to exist even for a short while. Blessed are You, Lord, Who heals all flesh and performs wonders.

The ancients who wrote the prayer books understood things about the human body that were not very well known outside the Jewish community. They codified them in the prayer book.

What is the point of reading this prayer every morning? Perhaps it is to remind us that every breath we take could be our last. It is supposed to humble us and make us understand that time is limited, that we're finite. We're flesh and blood, no matter how big we think we are.

Apparently, the prayer didn't work for Bernie Madoff. Neither does it seem to work for so many people walking around in religious garb. Maybe they don't read prayers like this one. Or they don't understand them. For how many people are prayers like these just mumbo jumbo? If they understood their significance, they wouldn't be stealing Medicare after putting on the outfit.

Prayers like this are supposed to stop the gonif who wears the black clothing and does the shuckling and still rips off Medicare. In many cases, even the religious don't believe what they read.

Years after discovering this prayer, I read something from a different religion, which said words to this effect: It doesn't really matter if you read the prayer book every day and perform all the rituals. What really matters to God is whether you are sincere in your belief in Him. That sincerity is the reality I'm talking about.

Maybe reality is nothing more than sincerity. I don't mean a con man's sincerity or putting on an act. There is enough of that in the world. Every great salesman is a con man. He pretends that he believes in what he's selling you. Maybe some do; maybe some don't. You can't prejudge everybody.

Think about all the fake movie stars with no talent whatsoever. They're surgically altered, like androids or bionic people. You don't know who's real anymore. You don't know what's real. Maybe some people don't need reality. Maybe they want someone who's altered and looks better. That's certainly another way to look at it, that the altered body is the better body.

The wisdom of the prudent is to look well to his way;

But the folly of fools is deceit.

—Proverbs 14:8

"Eternity, knowledge, and bliss, that is reality," said one caller. "To solve the problems of birth, old age, disease, and death, that's facing reality. Real reality is eternity, knowledge, and bliss because there is all this disease and death and birth that's forced upon us. Nobody wants it, because by nature we're eternal. We're full of knowledge, full of bliss. But we're all in the prison house of this material world. And that's reality."

The Buddhists believe the material world is a prison, an illusion. But I am not a Buddhist. I am reminded of a story I once heard about Einstein. I don't know if it's true. Shortly after he published his General Theory of Relativity, he agreed to an audience. He couldn't meet everyone, but he admitted a prominent man, who said to him, "Herr Einstein, I understand your theory of relativity. Everything is imaginary. It's all imagined."

The story goes that Einstein went up to the man, slapped him in the face, and asked, "Is that imagined?"

Reality is great to talk about until you fall off a ladder and break a leg. I remember when I was eighteen years old and going through my *Sorrows of Young Werther* phase. I didn't know who I was, where I was going, or what I was going to be. I was asking "What is life about? What is the meaning of existence?" and going through all the turmoil kids go through if they're sensitive or have a brain. I think everyone goes through this phase. The toughest person on earth asks these questions at some point in their life, usually during adolescence.

Some people can't get through that stage. They become drug addicts or alcoholics. They can't get past it because the answers are not there for them. They've lost faith or have no connection to faith. They don't believe in anything and don't know where to turn.

One day during that time in my life, I was driving through the Catskills and heard a *thunk* under the wheel of my car. I stopped, got out, and saw a dead rabbit. I went home that night and wrote a simple line in my journal: "Today, I ran over and killed a rabbit. This is reality."

Was that profound? It was to me. What I learned from running over that rabbit was that you can dream all you want, but at a certain point, when you run into a stone wall, you'll know what reality is. Or if someone punches you in the nose, you fall off a ladder, you see a baby being born, or you watch a parent suffer and die, you'll know what reality is. Trust me, reality has a way of kicking you in the behind.

———≻∘∘∘≺———

Trust in the LORD with all thy heart,

And lean not upon thine own understanding.

In all thy ways acknowledge Him,

And He will direct thy paths.

—Proverbs 3:5-6

———≻∘∘∘≺———

Where Is God?

Where is God? People seek to find God in as many places as there are on earth and in as many ways. I recall one of the pages from the great book *Zorba the Greek* by Nikos Kazantzakis. It's the story about a monk who climbs a mountain in Greece with the chief character, Zorba. And when they get to a certain point and they're relaxing, the priest tells Zorba a story about a woman he met in one of the villages. She was an outcast. She was a widow, and for some reason the people looked down upon her, thinking that she was a loose woman, so to speak.

The long and the short of it is the priest spent the night with her, had sex with her, probably for the first time in his life, and he told Zorba that when dawn came the following morning, he was closer to God than he had ever been in his life.

Well, that's one way people find God. I guess it's through transcendental experiences, whether they be sex, drugs, music, etc. People see God in their own way every day. Some people say they stand on a shoreline, listening to the waves pound against the shore, and feel closer to God. Or they walk on a beach or in a forest. There's that famous song from many years ago about hearing the cry of a newborn baby and knowing why you believe what you do.

Those are the ways people seek communion with the greater spirit to which we are all connected. After all, what are we? In addition to being the blood, the bone, the vessels, the tissue, we are spirit. And everything we come into contact with resonates on or with this spirit, for better or for worse. We know that some people can bring us down or give us a headache, some can bring us up, some can make us happy, some can make us sad, some can elevate us. What is that about?

It's about the fact that we're like tuning forks and we resonate with other energy forces. The other energy forces can be other people, a pounding surf, an animal, a dog, a cat, a bird. But the ultimate tuning fork in the sky is what we're talking about in this book. How can we tap into that resonance?

Some people go to church, and in joining a congregation, they are better able to resonate with the higher power. I remember when I was a young boy, I asked about my grandfather, who died long before I was born. The word came down that my grandfather was not a religious man, that he didn't go to a temple to pray. Instead, he said he could be out in nature with his back to a tree and talk to God. In many ways, the same is true for me today.

He that walketh with wise men shall be wise;

But the companion of fools shall smart for it.

—Proverbs 13:20

PART II.

GOD AND NATURE

Why did God create the world?

What is Man's role in creation?

Does God intervene, and how much?

What is the relationship between God and science?

I wrote this book because I decided to get closer to God again. I'm at the same phase of my life as I was decades ago, when I moved so far away from God and became so cynical that my life started to unravel in a certain way. My head started to unravel. And it was only by getting closer to God that I was able to get it all together again. That's when my life and career took off.

I wouldn't say that if it weren't true. It's not as though my life is unraveling again, but I wasn't feeling connected to the spiritual as much as I had before. And I wanted to be. I knew how to do it; I know who to be with; I know how to be there. It's an interesting story.

A few months back, before I was due to have some dental work done, I was in LA. I came back home and wasn't feeling good. I had the flu. On a Wednesday night, I had a dream that I was in a huge convocation of religious Jews. I was wandering around looking for a seat but couldn't find one. There were tens of thousands of people. It was an almost biblical setting. Everyone had a seat but me. Finally I found a seat and sat down.

The very next morning, I received an e-mail from one of the most prominent leaders of the Chabad orthodox religious group in America. I had rarely spoken with him previously; I think I had met him once. Out of the blue, he told me they were having a meeting the next day in Los Angeles of eighty of the top rabbis in California. I'm talking about the heavy-duty biblical guys. There were no other attendees who were not rabbis, but he was inviting me. I had no idea why they had thought of me.

I told him I considered it a high honor, but I couldn't go. I had just returned from LA and the next day had to go for a bone implant. So I didn't attend the conference, but I'm telling you, it was weird. I know that by my wanting to reach out to my spiritual road and get back to being connected with my spirituality, I must have contacted some kind of vibration in the universe that has come back down to this plane and had an immediate reverberation in my life.

That's how it works. Once you tune in or you contact the spiritual core of your own being, which resonates with the higher power, the higher power resonates back down to the earth and does things for us. I don't know. But I sense that that's how it works. There is a resonance factor.

The Amulet

A very special thing has occurred. I'm holding an amulet in my hand. Do you know what an amulet is? Christians, they don't believe in amulets. They think they're anti-God. They don't understand that some amulets bring you closer to God, not farther away. As I said before, for years Catholics in America had little plastic statues of St. Christopher in their cars. Then the statues gave way to dream catchers. That was the end of America as far as I knew it. Those statues were icon-effigies the Catholics had. That didn't make them less Catholic, did it? What about wearing a cross? Is that not a sort of amulet, a protection against evil? It is.

What I'm getting at is somewhat related to the St. Christopher medal thing. When Americans drove around in Dodge Darts and other big American cars in the 1970s, there were St. Christopher statues all over America. Suddenly we woke up in the 1990s and there were dream catchers hanging off the mirrors. Every girl in the Bay Area with chlamydia was driving around with a dream catcher, hoping the dream catcher would cure her. It didn't work.

A while back, I was somewhere I hadn't been in years. It was a house I used to live and work in. For sixteen years I had done radio shows out of that home. When I was a local host, it took me years to get the local station to permit me to do a remote broadcast out of my house. I had to argue and beg for it for years to let me put in a home studio. Then when I did, I wound up feeling more isolated than I ever had in my life, and I dreamed of being back at the radio station. There's something about the stink of the garbage can in the studio, the stink of perfume that people would leave there, that could blind you. One of the reasons I like a home studio is that I'm a germophobic person. I never got the flu in there. It's me and the dog. He doesn't get the flu.

So, after the renovation, I moved back into the old house and the old home studio. Naturally, things had been left there, including paintings, pictures, photographs, some of the curtains. I found stuff that I had long forgotten.

One night, I stayed there during a rainstorm. I wanted to be away from the Bay. It was too noisy, the pounding, crashing surf, wet and wild. In a box I had stored, I found an ivory object inscribed in Hebrew. The back was a cheap sort of metal, like silver, and there were tinkling things hanging from it.

I knew it was an amulet from the Middle East. I think I had bought it in Israel many years before. I had bought two of them, as a matter of fact. I don't even know what was on it. I remember when my mother was alive, I showed her the amulet. She never really related to anything I did. For some weird reason that I never understood until recently, she looked at that amulet and said, "That's very interesting that you brought that back from Israel. What is it?" She touched it, and I saw some electricity go through her. Until I found it again, I had forgotten about that. I had put the amulet aside. I had left it in a box and forgotten it.

One night, after returning from a pub, I ripped a muscle in my neck. I had hurt my neck years before, and a masseuse had almost destroyed it. I never let that woman near me again. She's a monster. I got over that; then I hurt the other side of my neck.

In the house I've been telling you about, there's an exercise machine. I hate exercise machines. They're inhuman. Normally, I confine my regimen to natural exercises such as push-ups, sit-ups, bicycling, etc. But for some weird reason I wanted to get into shape again, and I started pulling down on the pull-down bar on that inhuman machine. I must have ripped the muscle again. The pain was excruciating, but I wouldn't even take an aspirin for it. I'm stoic when it comes to that kind of pain. I don't want to start in with pills.

I looked at the amulet and said to myself, "Wait a minute, hold on. I don't believe in magic, but I believe in God." Was it a coincidence that I found that amulet from the Holy Land that I must have bought in 1978? I don't even remember exactly where I bought it. I think it was from a Yemenite peddler in a marketplace in Jerusalem. I bought two of them. As I say, my mother noted it, even though she was not very religious. But I know there's some kind of mystical streak in my family line on her side.

Many women have clairvoyant abilities, can see things others can't see. What gives them that extra power of seeing? Where does it come from? Well, it's inherent. It's genetic, okay. They inherited it, usually from their mother's line but not always. You can call it many things. If you work on the dark side, it's called witchcraft. If you work on the good side, it's not called witchcraft, right? Amulets of any kind can be put to either good or evil use.

Now, you may be a skeptical and very rational person who doesn't believe in any of this crap. You may say it's nonsense. But do you carry anything around with you for good luck? Do you carry anything on an airplane? Did any of you carry anything into battle that you believe protected you? That's what I'm talking about.

For many years I was into herbal medicine. For many years I wrote books on healing. I was in clinical practice as a healer for only a few years after I received my doctorate, from about 1978 to 1980 or '81. I wasn't ready for it then. Now if I get sick, I go only to medical doctors. I try to heal myself to avoid the need for modern medicine, but once I have an acute condition, I use modern medicine.

Obviously, I take tons of the right vitamins and use herbal medicine when I need to. I've always known, since I was a young man, that I have healing powers. Some of us have them, some don't. I don't mean clinical or technical, I'm talking about actual physical, spiritual healing powers. Now, I have avoided this part of my being for a long time, for many reasons. I don't want to wind up being accused of or becoming a fake guru. Let me be very clear about that. You can easily take your own Kool-Aid here, and you can wind up on a ranch in Antelope, Oregon, with twenty-five Rolls Royces and fifty women, and then have to flee the state for Denmark.

So I must be very careful of my own strengths and powers. You know and I know that in this world, but for the grace of God, you or I could have wound up a homeless person in the gutter, instead of who we are. Am I right or wrong? Do you think everything you have in your life, all the blessings you have, are there only because of yourself? It's because of God's power and will. I've known this all my life.

What I'm saying to you from my perspective is also true in reverse. That poor, unfortunate person in the street could have been you. It's a matter of chance. Things happen to people. Who can say what makes a person down on his luck or why something goes wrong in her life? Or why a child gets cancer? I can't. I have no knowledge about any of that.

Let me go back to the amulet I found. I bought two of them in Israel in the 1970s, put them aside, and paid no attention to them for decades. Then I found one right after I had pulled a muscle in my neck. I picked it up and said, "I know this thing has power." I put it on my neck and said, "I don't believe in magic, but I believe in God."

❧

> *A man also or a woman that divineth by a ghost or a familiar spirit, shall surely be put to death;*
>
> —Leviticus 20:27

❧

I stayed there in bed holding it to the muscle that was ripped. And I have to tell you from the bottom of my heart, the pain subsided within three to four minutes. It came back the next morning. I can hear the nonbelievers saying, "Ah, it's mind over matter, don't be stupid. Come on, you're a man of science, don't be a fool. What do you believe in that for?"

I decided that night that I'm going to keep trying this thing on people in my life who are sick. As I write this, I can feel the heat right now, because I just put it on my neck. I can feel the whole heat of my body in this thing. I know it has tremendous power. It's a secret thing.

I know these are Yemenite amulets. I can tell by the design of the jewelry and what's on the little hanging trinkets. Now, you never see Jews in America with this. They're modern Jews, they don't believe in any of this stuff. I don't know what they believe in, but that's their business. Each person's different.

One day, I called a rabbi known for mysticism and said, "I need to meet some rabbis who are into mysticism." I told him some problems I was having in my life, and I asked him to do something for me. He said, "No, Michael, you're so powerful. You're the rabbi. You have to do it for yourself." He said, "You speak to God."

Not long ago, I called him again. He was so excited to hear from me. I had sent him an e-mail picture of the amulet for him to translate the Hebrew. He said to me, "Michael, listen to what is written on the amulet in Hebrew. It's the blessing of Joseph. It says, 'You are my son, and the evil eye cannot hurt you. You are like the fish, and no evil eye can get to you. If you believe in God, no evil eye can touch you. When you get conceited, the evil eye can touch you.'"

He also said, "Tell all your listeners today that if they have had luck in their life and they are rich people or they're wealthy or they're doing well, to watch out for conceit. The minute they are filled with conceit, the evil eye will touch them." He continued, "This is the most important thing that I have to tell you, because it so happens that what you told me today about that amulet is, by coincidence, Michael, the exact weekly portion of the Torah to Jewish people. Passage 49:22, blessings of Joseph. Don't flaunt your wealth, or people will be jealous of you. You are my son, and the evil eye cannot hurt you. You are like the fish, and no evil eye can get you."

How Sensitive Do You
Want to Be?

There's a trend in America and the West now where people are overly sensitive to the living things around them. We all know about vegan diet. People think it's healthier. This is not a book about nutrition, so I won't get into that. But I do want to talk about people becoming so sensitive to animal life that they refuse to eat animals or animal products. I understand that. It would be hard to find many people who would not become vegetarians after visiting a slaughterhouse or watching a film of what happens inside a slaughterhouse, seeing the fear in the animals' eyes and hearing their cries as they're killed. I understand the sympathy people have for them.

But there are also people who say that they can hear the trees crying in a newly built home or a newly built cabin. I remember reading about this in a story by a rabbi of the Orthodox Jewish tradition Chabad, written sometime in the seventeenth century in Russia or Poland. One of the sages wrote that when he went into a newly built cabin, he could hear the trees it was made of cry. There's another story about the son of one of the great sages who took a leaf off a tree as he was walking in the forest with his father, and the father admonished him, saying, "How can you be so insensitive to ruin something that is so alive for no reason whatsoever?"

So how sensitive you want to be is the question. How tuned in do you want to be to the voices that travel around the world that no one can hear except the very few, the mad and the enlightened? And what are the voices that we're talking about? They can be anything. They can be the voices of people crying out as they die, the voices of spirits, things of that nature. How sensitive do you want to be is always the question.

In my own life, I do not think it's that important to tune in to such an extent that you lose the scope of the world in which we are living, the here and now, the world where our feet are planted on the ground. This earth is the only heaven for so many billions of people, and we must learn to live in this heaven God has created. Sure, there may be an afterlife, but we don't know that for sure. The only world we have direct knowledge of is this world, which we must not mess up. So how sensitive you want to be becomes not so much a question as a statement. Being insensitive makes you oafish, but being overly sensitive can render you incapable of living on this earth.

Dominion

According to Genesis, God told Adam and Eve:

> Be fruitful, and multiply, and replenish the earth, and subdue it; and have dominion over the fish of the sea, and over the fowl of the air, and over every living thing that creepeth upon the earth.

There are some things in the Bible I don't happen to agree with. Does it make me an anti-God, anti-religious person? No, I would say that people must evolve past the original message. I mean, we don't kill adulterers anymore, do we? Do we kill homosexuals? Not unless you're a retrograde, throwback Islamist. There are many things in the Bible that must be taken in the context of the times, and one of them is the passage I quoted above. What does "have dominion" really mean? Does it mean you should slaughter animals mercilessly and eat them? I don't think so. In fact, I interpret having dominion to mean protecting them.

I know I'm not alone because I talk to people of all belief systems, political and spiritual, every day on *The Savage Nation*. I particularly remember a caller who shared my interpretation of dominion. She thanked me for sharing it and said, "I think when

And God said: 'Let us make man in our image, after our likeness; and let them have dominion over the fish of the sea, and over the fowl of the air, and over the cattle, and over all the earth, and over every creeping thing that creepeth upon the earth.'

— Genesis 1:26

you love God, you love all of His creatures and His creations. And I am so glad that you talked about this today."

We must understand there comes a point in human evolution when we must evolve in our observations about not only ourselves or the earth or the cosmos but about animals, too. They're not all there for our pleasure or just to kill and eat them. That's not what having dominion means.

We have dominion over many things that we don't necessarily consume to the point of destroying them. What do you think crop rotation is for? What about your car? You don't drive it as fast as it goes or beat it up by taking curves fast or peeling out when the light turns green. That's not just because you might get a ticket. It's also because you need that car to last a long time. Therefore, you forgo the pleasure of pushing it to its limit every time you drive it so it will be there for you next year and the year after.

That's called *conservation*. I wrote in *Trump's War* about why conservation is a core conservative political principle that modern conservatives should reclaim. Well, I have news for you. It's a core spiritual concept as well, which is directly related to the passage in Genesis about having dominion over the earth and its living inhabitants.

I remember another caller who echoed the political side of this argument on my show. She told me, "I liked your comment. I liked you bringing up the environmental issue because you're right. Many Republicans, many conservatives do not talk about this issue. Um, it's passed off and people turn their nose up at it, but it is very important because this earth is all that we have."

It's not inconsistent for a person to be a political conservative and a conservationist. In fact, they're unified. They're brother-and-sister issues. Conservation is not an issue that should be controlled by the so-called radical Left. We should control that issue. But the brother and sister have another sibling, the soul. Being a conservationist is truly the way to follow God's command in Genesis to exercise dominion over all living things.

One of the callers I referred to had a classical education and had studied Latin. She said she had learned Latin "growing up," which means she may have been home schooled. I don't know. But she made a very important point. She said she believed that the word *dominion* in the Bible came from the Latin word *dominus*, which translates literally as "lord" or "master." She said, "That can mean caretaker, that can mean protector."

That's precisely what I'm talking about in terms of the relationship between dominion and conservation. God is our Lord and Master, but He doesn't hurt or destroy us for His own pleasure. On the contrary, He created the universe, the natural laws, above all reason, for precisely the opposite reasons. He wanted to allow us to thrive, to grow, to maximize our potential happiness. He gave us free will knowing we would often act contrary to His wishes, but without which we could not achieve goodness or happiness.

There is a correlation between God's dominion over us and our dominion over plants and animals. It is not a direct, one-to-one correlation. Just as we are made in God's image but are not gods ourselves, so, too, is our dominion over animals analogous to God's dominion over us, but not equal. God does not need to consume us to survive as we need to consume living things to survive.

That's right, we need to consume living things, either plants or animals, to survive. We can't live on dirt. Sometimes I wonder if our psychotic liberal friends even admit that to themselves. That is another point on which political conservatism, conservation, and God's Word all converge. This physical world is imperfect, as we are imperfect. We cannot achieve the sublime perfection of Heaven on Earth. But we can strive for it, understanding that perfection is impossible.

That means that we must eat plants and animals to survive but we don't have to destroy whole species just because we can. It is in our best interest to conserve them for the future. That is the true meaning of exercising dominion: to ensure that all living things have the opportunity to flourish, which will allow human beings to benefit from them in the future. In doing so, we enable them to live the best life they possibly can in a world in which living things must consume other living things to survive. And we must not make them suffer when they are slaughtered. That, by the way, is the origin of the kosher food laws: to teach man, among other things, to be compassionate to animals and the earth.

And I brought you into a land of fruitful fields, to eat the fruit thereof and the good thereof; but when ye entered, ye defiled My land, and made My heritage an abomination.

—Jeremiah 2:7

Woe is me! for I am as the last
of the summer fruits,

As the grape gleanings of the vintage;

There is no cluster to eat;

Nor first-ripe fig which my soul desireth.

The godly man is perished out of the earth,

And the upright among men is no more;

— Micah 7:1–2

First Fruits

I've yet to tell you about the first fruit of the season. It's biblical to me. I have a small property north of San Francisco on which I have an orchard. When I bought it in 2002, it had a peach orchard on it that eventually died off. I don't know the reason; perhaps some disease.

Eventually I put in a new orchard. It's not a lot of trees, maybe fifteen or twenty, I'm not sure exactly how many. But I take such pride in and care for them. When I planted them a few years ago, they were just baby saplings, like when you first buy them from a nursery.

One day, my gardener came down to one of the places I broadcast from and said, "Michael, here are the first peaches that we picked for you." They were little peaches; I ate a few.

Why am I telling you this story? Because nature goes on no matter who is president, no matter what madness or filth you see on television. Nature is eternal. It keeps renewing itself. That's why we love our pets, our orchards, our connections to nature. It's why you love to go camping. It's why you love to go skiing.

I love my little peach orchard. That day, I got its first fruits. Look up "first fruits" in the Bible. You'll see what I mean.

PART III.

SCRIPTURES

But with righteousness shall he judge the poor,

And decide with equity for the meek of the land;

And he shall smite the land with the rod
of his mouth,

And with the breath of his lips shall he
slay the wicked.

And righteousness shall be the girdle of his loins,

And faithfulness the girdle of his reins.

— Isaiah 11:4–5

Why did God inspire the scriptures?

Should the scriptures be taken literally or viewed as myth/allegory?

What are the similarities/differences between Judeo-Christian scriptures and other holy writings?

I 'm an Old Testament kind of guy. I believe in the real McCoy. It's a pretty violent book. It's very powerful. Of course, we don't take the Old Testament literally. If we did, we'd probably all be slaughtered by rock throwers. But there is a lot of wisdom in it, based upon common sense in some ways, in logic in some ways. But it's seen by the atheists as a red light to their libido.

In plain English, the reason the hedonists hate religion and hate God is because they see them as holding up a red light to their hedonism. It says, "You shall not do this" and "You shall not do that." They want to do anything they want to. Fornicating with animals is fine because "if it feels good, do it." Why not do it in the road? That's their modus operandi. And we know what it's led to.

I believe there is going to be a rejuvenation of faith in this nation, a return to religion. I've already seen it in some ways. And just because these so-called elites, sneering snot noses in the media, do not show you what is going on, that does not mean it is not going on. And I feel it. In that sense, I'm not a rationalist; I'm an intuitivist. I can feel a change in this country. I believe this long highway of pollution has come to an end and will wind up in the trash heap.

The days that led here go back to a pornography case decided by the Supreme Court. That is what dumped the trash into everyone's neighborhood. That's what dumped pornography into everyone's corner. When so-called progressives took the First Amendment to mean that they could pump filth of the lowest and most degrading kind into every mind, that was the beginning of the end of American morality.

Believe me, there is a very big place in this country for a moralist and a reformist to come along, and I don't think we're going to get that out of a politician.

ᖋ

And the sun stood still, and the moon stayed,

Until the nation had avenged themselves of their enemies.

—Joshua 10:13

Reverend Jerry Falwell Debates Michael Savage

A while back, I had the opportunity to interview my friend, and great defender of what I believe in, Jerry Falwell. I really wanted to get his perspective on several issues I knew I would be wrestling with in this book. One of them was the crucifixion. I asked him, "Reverend, what does the crucifixion mean? To me it means if you crucify others, you crucify yourself. Does that analysis hold any water with you?"

Reverend Falwell replied, "That certainly can be an interpretation, but the ultimate meaning of the Cross is that God so loved the world and everyone in it: black, white, red, yellow, Jew, gentile, rich, poor. God so loved the world that he gave his only begotten son, Christ, to die on that cross to pay our sin debt in full forever, and only perfect God, perfect man, in one person could do that."

Here's the part I don't understand: How could Jesus die for all man's sins for all time when such evil exists? Does that exonerate them? Does that exonerate a child rapist? Throughout this book, I've been talking about personal responsibility. Over and over, we've seen examples of how it is each individual who must seek out God and do His work. Everyone must atone for his own sins.

For My people is foolish,

They know Me not;

They are sottish children,

And they have no understanding;

They are wise to do evil,

But to do good they have no knowledge.

— Jeremiah 4:22

So it makes no sense to me that Jesus could have done anything to atone for the sins of a murderer who killed yesterday.

Reverend Falwell replied, "Because first of all He is the Son of God and God the Son, perfect man, perfect God. Theologians refer to Him as the God Man, and because He is the God Man He was able to take it upon Himself. Only God could do that. In that efficacious way, the sins of everyone from Adam to the last person that shall ever be born upon this earth, past, present, future. When He said it is finished on the cross, it meant just that: I paid the debt in full; I've satisfied my heavenly father. My blood is shed; I've risen now from the dead. Alive forevermore, and all who trust Me shall have everlasting life. The death of Christ is sufficient to save all men everywhere. It is sufficient to save only those who believe and receive Him."

For me, that begged another obvious question, which is "Can a non-Christian be saved?" What if someone is not a murderer, is not a rapist, in fact lives an exemplary life, but is not a Christian? What if Mother Teresa had lived a life identical to the one she lived but had been a Buddhist? Would she be saved? What about a Jewish man who reads the Bible every day, attends the synagogue, loves his fellow man, and avoids sin as well as the best of Christians? Can that man be saved?

My friend answered according to his faith and his convictions. He quoted the Bible, saying, "'He that hath the Son hath life; and he that hath not the Son of God hath not life,' but the wrath of God abides upon him. One must receive Christ. That's not anti-Semitic; it's not anti-gentile. There are many Baptists who have not received Christ. They may be church members and have been baptized but have never personally received the atonement: Christ's death, burial, resurrection for our sins as Lord and Savior."

Of course, I cannot be completely satisfied with that answer, but people of goodwill can disagree on these matters. That was the real reason for the First Amendment. It wasn't to ban God from the public square. That's a liberal perversion of the First Amendment. The First Amendment sought to protect every individual's right to believe and worship as he saw fit. The founders believed that because no one can know the answers to these ultimate questions, every individual has an inalienable right to decide for himself what the answers are. He can't be forced to go against his beliefs by a national religion. That's what the First Amendment and the inalienable right of conscience it protects really means.

Good people of any faith should be respected. We cannot dismiss the billions of people on Earth who are not Christian. What about the Native Americans, who do not even believe in an all-powerful God? Should we say all of them are pagans not worthy of salvation if they do not convert to Christianity?

I see God as the center of a spiritual wheel, with all the spokes being the many religions and beliefs that lead to God.

❦

And Moses chose able men out of all Israel, and made them heads over the people, rulers of thousands, rulers of hundreds, rulers of fifties, and rulers of tens.

—Exodus 18:25

Exodus 18:21

Turning to Exodus, the first chapter and verse I marked was 18:21, where it says, "Moreover, thou shalt provide out of all the people able men, such as fear God, men of truth, hating unjust gain; and place such over them to be rulers of thousands, rulers of hundreds, rulers of fifties, and rulers of tens." Verse 25–6 continue, "And Moses chose able men out of all Israel and made them heads over the people, rulers of thousands, rulers of hundreds, rulers of fifties, and rulers of tens. And they judged the people at all seasons. The hard causes they brought unto Moses but every small matter, they judged themselves."

What does this mean to me? It means that in every generation going back to Moses, we have always sought God-fearing men who love the truth, who hate thieves. And we elect them to positions of power. Where does that leave us today?

Honour thy father and thy mother, that thy days may be long upon the land which the LORD thy God giveth thee.

Thou shalt not murder.

Thou shalt not commit adultery.

Thou shalt not steal.

Thou shalt not bear false witness against thy neighbour.

Thou shalt not covet thy neighbour's house; thou shalt not covet thy neighbour's wife, nor his man-servant, nor his maid-servant, nor his ox, nor his ass, nor any thing that is thy neighbour's.

— Exodus 20:12–14

Exodus—The Ten Commandments

The next passage I marked is Exodus 20:12–14. It's about the Ten Commandments and begins with, "Honor thy father and thy mother that thy days may be long upon the land which the Lord thy God giveth thee."

What does that really mean? For those of us who have had trouble with one or both of our parents, does it mean we must worship them? As a very thoughtful religious woman, who herself had had continuous problems with her mother, told me a long time ago, no, it does not mean blind worship of your parents. It means you should honor that you come from your father and your mother. That gives us a concept of belonging, of an origin, of who we are as beings, that we were not born unto ourselves. It does not mean we must worship our father and our mother, especially if we have a very difficult relationship with them.

As for the other commandments, do they not speak for themselves? 20:13 says, "Thou shalt not murder." The Hebrew word is very interesting. It says "murder," not "kill." You are permitted to kill in war, in self-defense. Murder is quite different from kill. Think about it.

We don't have to define the others: thou shalt not commit adultery, thou shalt not steal, thou shalt not bear false witness against thy neighbor, thou shalt not covet thy neighbor's house, thou shalt not not covet thy neighbor's wife, nor his manservant, nor his maidservant, nor his ox, nor his ass, nor anything that is thy neighbor's. They're all self-explanatory. The two most interesting words in the passage are those regarding murder as opposed to killing and the concept of what honor thy father and thy mother means.

The child shall behave insolently against the aged,

And the base against the honourable,

For a man shall take hold of his brother of the house of his father:

'Thou hast a mantle,

Be thou our ruler,

And let this ruin be under thy hand.'

—Isaiah 3:5–6

An Eye for an Eye

Exodus contains all sorts of rules about an eye for an eye, which are self-explanatory. We don't live in an eye-for-an-eye world, and many of us feel that the justice system is flawed because punishments don't fit the crimes. It seems to most of us that the true criminals are not punished sufficiently.

For example, Exodus 21:26 says, "If a man smite the eye of his bondman or the eye of his bondwoman and destroy it, he shall let him go free for his eye's sake. And if he smite out his bondman's tooth or his bondwoman's tooth, he shall let him go free for his tooth's sake."

What does that mean? It means an eye for an eye, more or less. It says to give them freedom to compensate for injury. Is that an eye for an eye?

Earlier, in 21:22, it says if men are working together and hurt a pregnant woman, they must pay a fine. But if they accidentally kill the baby, it says, ". . . if any harm follow then thou shalt give life for life, eye for eye, tooth for tooth, hand for hand, foot for foot, burning for burning, wound for wound, strike for strike."

Do we want to live in such a world? No, we don't. Do we want to live in Saudi Arabia, where they cut the hands off thieves? Some of us would say yes; I would say no. On the other hand, when we

And if men strive together, and hurt a woman with child, so that her fruit depart, and yet no harm follow, he shall be surely fined, according as the woman's husband shall lay upon him; and he shall pay as the judges determine.

— Exodus 21:22

live in a world that is ruled by liberal judges, where the courts are run by liberal lawyers, where there does not seem to be much punishment for some crimes, we're all asking ourselves how we can make the pendulum swing to a more equitable justice system. That's my interpretation of Exodus and where we are today.

But if any harm follow, then thou shalt give life for life, eye for eye, tooth for tooth, hand for hand, foot for foot, burning for burning, wound for wound, stripe for stripe.

—Exodus 21:23–25

And the man said: 'This is now bone of my bones, and flesh of my flesh; she shall be called Woman, because she was taken out of Man.'

Therefore shall a man leave his father and his mother, and shall cleave unto his wife, and they shall be one flesh.

And they were both naked, the man and his wife, and were not ashamed.

— Genesis 2:23–25

The Garden of Eden

In Genesis, He writes this. He, God. You know who He is? God. It's not Barack Obama. He. Not Obama. Not Castro, not Stalin, not Lenin. Not any of your heroes. Not Karl Marx, not George Soros, but He, God. God wrote the Bible, starting with Genesis, the first book of Moses, so to speak. And in Genesis 2:18, He says, "And the Lord God said it is not good that the man should be alone. I will make him a help meet for him."

Then it talks about how He created all the other animals and what Adam would call them. He gave names to the cattle and the fowl of the air and to every beast of the field. Then He looked around and said, but for Adam there was not found a help meet for him. And so He caused a deep sleep to fall upon the man. "And He took one of his ribs and closed up the place with flesh instead thereof. And the rib which the Lord God had taken from the man, made He a woman, and brought her unto the man. And the man said, 'This is now bone of my bones and flesh of my flesh. She shall be called woman because she was taken out of man.'"

Now listen to the rest of this. Listen to it as poetry. "Therefore shall a man leave his father and his mother, and shall cleave unto his wife, and they shall be one flesh. And they were both naked, the man and his wife, and were not ashamed." I could spend an entire book on that one passage from Genesis, but I don't think it takes an entire book to show that since the beginning of recorded history, all religions have recognized that it's man and woman, that there's no need for a third-sex bathroom. You have mental problems? You're not sure who you are? We're sorry for you. We're not going to hurt you. We accept you, but please don't twist our children's minds.

Every culture, every religion, every people on the planet, every dog, every cat, every mouse, every bird, every pigeon, everything on Earth understands that, except for the people in San Francisco. As I read a thing like that, I look further. And that's usually when I turn to the Rock of Ages.

It's not that I believe every word. I'm not a biblical absolutist, but it's been around for thousands of years. Of course, everyone is not as smart as the current crop of know-it-all equalizers, I understand that. The poor people who believed in God and the Bible all these years, they just didn't have the brains of Obama and the other atheists around him, but they did the best they could.

We know what Sodom and Gomorrah are. The story has metaphorical power. "Then the Lord caused rain upon Sodom and Gomorrah, brimstone and fire from the Lord out of Heaven. And he overthrew those cities and all the plain, and all the inhabitants of the cities and that which grew upon the ground. But [Lot's] wife looked back from behind him, and she became a pillar of salt." From that biblical phrase came the statement "Don't look back." Remember the Bob Dylan song and the movie *Don't Look Back*?

I'm impressed with how much great literature is based upon biblical stories, or biblical truths, if you want to put it that way. I know it sounds suspicious, but I got weirdly teary reading about Cain and the part about east of Eden. I can't put my finger on it.

*T*hen the LORD caused to rain upon Sodom

and upon Gomorrah brimstone and fire from the

LORD out of heaven; and He overthrow those cities,

and all the Plain, and all the inhabitants

of the cities, and that which grew upon the ground.

But his wife looked back from behind him,

and she became a pillar of salt.

— Genesis 19:24–26

I wish I could. It moved me because of the power of the words of the Bible.

When you think about the three great religions on earth, Judaism, Christianity, and Islam, they are three religions that are fundamentally tied by one common thread: monotheism, the belief in a single God. Forget about the Wahhabis who have infected Islam. Forget about the fact that Saudi Arabia has poisoned Islam, at least for the moment. If you look at the purity of Islam and you denude Islam of its hatred, of the killing and the murdering of infidels, there is so much beauty in all three religions. And they all come from the same source, which is the belief in God.

East of Eden

If you ask even the most uneducated person you know about the Garden of Eden, they know what you're talking about. Everyone knows what the Garden of Eden is. The minute you say it, they get an image. It may mean different things to different people.

But there is another place, east of Eden, referenced in the Bible, which is the Land of Nod. That's funny, because junkies say he nodded out. People say you want to nod off. Where does the word *nod* come from? How does that refer to someone nodding off or nodding out?

Well, the Book of Genesis in the Hebrew Bible says that there's a place east of Eden, where Cain was exiled by God after he had murdered his brother, Abel. He was sent from the Garden of Eden to a place called Nod. Genesis 4:16 says, "And Cain went out from the presence of the Lord and dwelt in the Land of Nod, east of Eden."

What does that mean, the Land of Nod? *Nod* is the Hebrew root of the verb "to wander." So if you live in the Land of Nod, that means you are a wandering person. You are a castoff. The wandering Jew lives in Nod. Of course, the colloquial meaning of the word *nod* in English is to fall asleep, to nod off. If you say,

"That person's going to the Land of Nod," that means he or she is going to sleep.

Genesis 4:17 says that "After arriving in the Land of Nod, Cain's wife bore him a son, Enoch, in whose name he built the first city." It's fascinating to me. There are places named after the Land of Nod. There are popular culture references, such as John Steinbeck's famous novel *East of Eden*. Two of its central themes are the betrayal of a brother and a land of sleep.

And Cain went out from the presence of the LORD,

and dwelt in the land of Nod, on the east of Eden.

—Genesis 4:16

Genesis 2:5 and 2:8

I have some brief comments on Genesis 2:5 and 2:8. Genesis 2:5 says, "No shrub of the field was yet on the earth and no herb of the field had yet sprung up." Genesis 2:8 says, "And the Lord God planted a garden eastward in Eden and there he put the man whom he had formed."

As I first read that, I shuddered when I thought of the great literature that has been derived from biblical statements. Of course you know that *East of Eden* came directly from the Bible. There are so many other literary references to the Bible by Shakespeare and other great writers over the ages, all derived from the greatest poet of all.

Genesis 2:18

And the Lord God said, "It is not good that the man should be alone." It's clear to anyone who reads it that man and woman belong together. I felt it necessary to repeat that point, given this age of ambivalence, but it seems to me that the universal truth for all mankind is man plus woman as one flesh. Period. End of story.

From Tennis to
Temple's Tempest

Lean, spare, and athletic, Barry is a sixty-year-old who looks better than most fit forty-year-olds. I would like to have met Barry on the tennis court where he taught professional players the psychology of winning. But I met him in a different setting, and as we talked, I was impressed by his being a learned rabbi and trained psychologist, not exhibiting the binds or trappings of either role, choosing instead the easy grace of master tennis instructor.

Fourteen years after I scented my first perfumed plumeria, heard the song of the dove, and was awed by great vertical rainbows in the tropical forest, I found myself in a hotel room on an island, witnessing the unshackling of my imprisoned other self.

My only son, Russell Goldencloud, was now twelve. In May of that year, he would walk to the Torah and read his portion before an assembly of his parents' friends.

I had avoided formal Judaism in my many intermediary years of wandering far from the fold, but Jewish I was. Jewish he would be, too. A member of sisterhoods and brotherhoods, paid tickets to worship on "high" holy days? Never!

My deceased grandfather Samuel, the father of my father, Benjamin, had taught me from his grave. His daughter, Beulah, my strong-willed aunt, had told me years after his premature death that he, too, had not believed in formal religion. "If you are in the woods, a tree to your back becomes a temple."

Pantheism? The worship of natural phenomena, such as the plumeria and rainbow? Perhaps. But who created those natural wonders?

And so it went, and so I went, and so went the religious teaching of my son, until I found myself on that tropical island in a paradisiacal corner of the universe with a free copy of *The Teaching of Buddha* in my hotel bedroom drawer.

Where the Gideons walked, the Buddhists now flew, placing the words of their teacher to encourage resistance against temptation, I suppose. But with a son, a daughter, and a loyal woman of fourteen years all sleeping wind-soft sleep in tropical beds adjacent to mine, where was the temptation?

The second night, unable to sleep, I drew the spare bed to the terrace and lay awake, the crashing surf both sedating and arousing me.

Here was purity, I thought. Yet visions of flooding waves running over this corner of the island disallowed the deep rest I so anxiously sought to soothe my aching lungs and heart, prematurely worn from life on the freeways of ambition.

In the sharp light by my bed, now snapped on, I restlessly pushed aside the five or six other books I had so greedily bought in the Honolulu bookstore: a biography of George Orwell and four or five English translations of modern Japanese novels.

Instead, the words of more ancient masters seemed to ring truer. I flipped through the pages of the small, colorfully jacketed book I had found in the bedroom drawer.

A man who chases after fame and wealth and love affairs is like a child who licks honey from the blade of a knife. While he is tasting the sweetness of honey, he has to risk hurting his tongue. He is like a man who carries a torch against a strong wind; the flame will surely burn his hands and face.

"The Way of Purification" was the section in *The Teaching of Buddha* where I found this cajoling jewel of instruction.

Without *insisting* on my good behavior this book immediately *felt like* the advice of a good friend! It *suggested* without telling me it "suggested."

As the waves continued to crash a hundred yards from that room,[1] I continued to read in the little portable bed out on the deck as my family slept their sleep and dreamed their dreams. Compared with my struggles with the world of books and words, the prim little volume found in the hotel room drawer seemed to answer so many needs.

---

[1] One week later, a fierce storm struck the island, washing that very room out to sea!

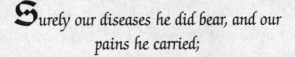

Surely our diseases he did bear, and our
pains he carried;

Whereas we did esteem him stricken,

Smitten of God, and afflicted.

—Isaiah 53:4

A Covenant with All
the Ills of the World

The connections I saw between the two lifeways, Buddhism and Judaism, were immediate and apparent.

The "six holes" which cause the loss of wealth are desire for intoxicating drinks and behaving foolishly, staying up late at night and losing the mind in frivolity, indulging in musical and theater entertainments, gambling, associating with evil companions, and neglecting one's duties. —BUDDHA

Rabbi Dosa,[2] the son of Horkinas, said, "Morning sleep and midday wine, and children's talk, and attending the houses of assembly of the ignorant, drive a man from the world." —JUDAH

---

[2] He was a wealthy man and wrote these words as a guide for his social equals.

Of course, there was a difference in the *style* of teaching. Where the Asian sages vaguely cajoled, the rabbis seemed to scold. Or, as in the next set, I found the Buddhist verse more poetic and therefore more appealing.

Rain falls, winds blow, plants bloom, leaves mature and are blown away, these phenomena are all interrelated with causes and conditions, are brought about by them, and disappear as the causes and conditions change.

One is born through the conditions of parentage; his body is nourished by food; his spirit is nurtured by teaching and experience.

As a net is made up by a series of ties, so everything in this world is connected by a series of ties. If anyone thinks that the mesh of a net is an independent, isolated thing, he is mistaken. —Buddha

The Jewish teaching regarding cause and effect that I read as a child went like this. Note the similarity of *meaning* to the previous, Buddhist teaching. Rabbi Chananya said:

They that are born are destined to die; and the dead to be brought to life again; and the living to be judged, to know, to make known, and to be made conscious that He is God, He the Maker, He the Creator, He the Discerner, He the Judge, He the Witness, He the Complainant; He it is that will in future judge. Blessed be He, with whom there is no unrighteousness, nor forgetfulness, nor respect of persons, nor taking of bribes. Know also that everything is according to the reckoning, and let not thy imagination give thee hope that the grave will be a place of refuge for thee; . . . for perforce thou wilt in the future have to give account and reckoning before the Supreme King of kings, the Holy One.

I had long known God is a vengeful God, one who judged according to His laws, allowing no mercy. Nothing occurs on this earth that is not somehow related to behavior in this world or the world of our karmic past.

I had been taught that precept in two distinctly different ways by two distinctly different parents. My father, Benjamin, the son of Samuel, had given me the mechanistic view of the universe through his explanations of the natural world.

I remember Frank Buck, the animal collector, from a film shown in a cozy room one rainy summer day. I think it was in August, and my father was enjoying his intermittent summer rest from the antiques shop. The city was a hundred miles beyond the low round mountains that sheltered our precious togetherness. As the old projector flipped its filmic images of a far-off Indian jungle, with the pith-helmeted hero-collector trying to ensnare rare animals *without killing them*, my father whispered his running comments in that deep strong voice I still seek. He, as my first teacher, seemed to instruct me in a wisdom I immediately understood.

As an adult, I have learned that *as a person I take things personally.* Those proclaiming the wisdom of the East declare the opposite. They believe that the precept of "humility" requires a loss of personhood, a willingness to submit to others who may insult, even humiliate them.

Somehow, Frank Buck's ensnarement of those poor wild beasts in the Indian jungle, in that rainy summer movie room, showed me the supremacy of man over beast, *with mercy*. All men seek to control others who cannot control themselves. That passion is the wild beast, and our "will" or belief in self-control is the pathway to reason, to compassion, and to God. (But what troubles I *would* have, still *do* have, in controlling my desires!)

My mother, Rachel, daughter of Rebecca, accepted man's fate more pacifically. Her ill son, my brother Jerome, the blond-haired, blue-eyed beauty, had been born blind, deaf, and unable to move. He was the ultimate hostage in a game between God and the family.

"Why? Oh, why," I used to ask this patient woman, "did God, who you say is good, make Jerome so broken?"

Despite her tears, her permanently handkerchiefed hand, her loyalty to her second son, my poor brother, was boundless.

"God," she told me, "never makes a mistake. He has His reasons for everything."

And so she accepted her imperfect son, continuing to visit him once a week for twenty-three long, cold years after he had been sent to a hospital, against her maternal instinct, at the advice of a secular physician, "for the sake of the healthy children."

"The healthy children" were myself and my sister. As time would prove, the silent may be wiser than those capable of ensnaring with their guile; the crippled lither than the athlete.

Which is why I searched for the answers in the distant silence of the Pacific islands, seeking to find the cure for my little brother, long dead, in a covenant with all the ills of the world.

The Power of the Searcher

I am not the first Jew to walk with Buddha at my side. My son's rabbi told me about Martin Buber's affinity for this combination. But the great Jewish philosopher's infatuation with the inner, self-centered orientation of that other religion came to an abrupt end. One day, a young student came to see him and asked many questions. The older man, growing impatient with the distraction, ended the interview abruptly. The boy left and soon afterward committed suicide.

Buber assumed responsibility, saying afterward that he'd answered all the boy's questions except the one left unasked. That sad incident convinced him that the self-centered inner life of reflection suggested by the teachings of Buddha was inferior to the outward world way of active dialogue, a basic Jewish proclivity.

Rabbi Chanina used to say, "He whose deeds exceed his wisdom, his wisdom shall endure; but he whose wisdom exceeds his deeds, his wisdom will not endure."

Passion's Power

Of course, things are not as clear cut as "action" versus "inaction," "inner" versus "outer," "monologue" versus "dialogue," and so on. Both religions seem to teach the same things: namely, control the passions, clear the mind, do good deeds.

> If a man's body and mind are under control he should give evidence of it in virtuous deeds. This is a sacred duty. Faith will then be his wealth, sincerity will give his life a sweet savor, and to accumulate virtues will be his sacred task. —BUDDHA

Ben Zoma[3] said:

> Who is wise? He who learns from all men. . . . Who is mighty? He who subdues his passions. . . . Who is rich? He who rejoices in his portion. . . . Who is worthy of honor? He who respects his fellow-man.

---

[3] "Ben Zoma's four questions and answers, sublime in their simplicity, are among the most noteworthy gnomic sayings in religious literature" (unknown source).

Hillel, one of my favorite teachers, used to say:

An empty-handed man cannot be a sin-fearing man, nor
can an ignorant person be truly pious, nor can the diffi-
dent learn, nor the passionate teach, nor is everyone who
excels in business wise. In a place where there are no men,
strive to be a man.

But life *cannot* be lived simply by coining or memorizing
wise sayings. The trap in which I found myself was the result of
inheriting a "hot" nature, for which I sought the cure and calm of
an objective wisdom. Drawn to the burning flames life offered, I
would obey my desires up to a point, only to step back, partly satisfied, never jumping whole-soulfully into the fire of chance.

Just as the pure and fragrant lotus flower grows out of the
mud of a swamp rather than out of the clean loam of an
upland field, so from the muck of worldly passions springs
the pure Enlightenment. . . . Even the mistaken views of
heretics and the delusions of worldly passions may be the
seeds of Buddhahood. —BUDDHA

Was it not my "passionate" nature that led me to search for
peace? Therefore, I realized at once that, without passion, peace
is meaningless. Without war, what meaning is there in the state
known as peace? It is the same for "good" and "evil," the corner-
stones of my training from toilet to temple. Why try to be good
when bad is just the dark side of this sphere? Can a moon always
shine, or must it, too, go into its dark phases, eventually disappearing from view, *still being a whole*, though it is out of sight?

This is how we turn: from our light phases to our dark; from hot to mild to cold; from wise to foolish, kind to cruel, happy to unhappy.

The principal value of religious teachings, then, from a personal or happiness point of view, is to smooth the transitions, making the changes less jarring to ourselves and others, allowing us to become an integrated or unified person.

To try to eliminate passion altogether is not only impossible but ultimately criminal or against the stream of life. Which teaching, then, would give me the greater happiness, the greater gift—the ability to keep alive my fiery nature without dashing myself onto the rocks below or hurting those around me? More, would I continue to laugh and make others release their bonds as I had done since childhood, long before I ever heard of the word *religion*?

> There are three kinds of people in the world. The first are those who are like letters carved in rock; they easily give way to anger and retain their angry thoughts for a long time. The second are those who are like letters written in sand; they give way to anger also, but their angry thoughts pass quickly away. The third is those who are like letters written in running water; they do not retain their passing thoughts; they let abuse and uncomfortable gossip pass by unnoticed; their minds are always pure and undisturbed.
> —DHARMA

> There are four kinds of tempers: he whom it is easy to provoke and easy to pacify, his loss disappears in his gain; he whom it is hard to provoke and hard to pacify, his gain

disappears in his loss; he who is hard to provoke and easy to pacify is a saint; he who is easy to provoke and hard to pacify is a wicked man. —Anonymous

For thou art a holy people unto the LORD thy God: the LORD thy God hath chosen thee to be His own treasure, out of all peoples that are upon the face of the earth.

— Deuteronomy 7:6

Lotus from the Muck

I began as a Buddhist, formless. In time, shaped as I was by my parents, my sister, even by my sacrificed brother, Jerome, "Jewish" became my identity as a cultural being. But what was this "religion" I belonged to? Was it merely candles flaming me to sleep on Friday eves like two golden rails if you quietly drifted off in your father's lap, squinting up long enough to distort the twin flames? Was it great, festive meals once or twice a year, the women cooking, seemingly forever, great filling dishes that I now know to be dreadfully unhealthful? Was it a cheap blue suit with other boys in like outfits walking to synagogue on our atonement day, dodging the "goyim" who chased us with nylon stockings filled with powdered chalk, swinging their mother's discarded skins to defile our once-a-year best and tell us we were Jews?

Defined so by *others*, I grew up Jewish, or so I thought.

Coming upon myself some forty years into life's endlessness, approaching my own cherished boy's initiation into his people, and again reevaluating my life as a Jew, I found religion to be the *least* important facet of the diamond!

Judaism is both more and less than *a* religion; both more and less than *a* people; surely not *a* land; and certainly not *a* way of life.

It is *more* than a religion when mere observance is transcended and seen for the God-binding acts they are, the rituals designed to bind us through the *shakras* and *shekinas*. It is *less* than a religion when dumb unthinkingness refuses to budge from its shelled camouflage.

It is more than a people; it is many peoples, from Yemenites, brown in hue, to Nordic-looking Germans. It is less than a people when the world or inner imbalance drives us to a collective act of madness.

It is more than a land; it is many lands; but beyond a geographical naturalism.

Wondering and worrying, I sat in my car in the rain, parked up a San Francisco hill. Looking back down Grant Avenue through the raindropped mirror, I heard the thought, "Where am I? What am I doing here? I used to be so sure of my place and direction." Soon after followed this rejoinder: "Didn't we all!"

The lights of a city, created and creating a sense of place. Today we belong to *this* place, yesterday to that, and tomorrow to the worlds of the deathless moons.

. . . from the muck of worldly passions springs the pure enlightenment. —DHARMA

But now, O LORD, Thou art our Father;

We are the clay, and Thou our potter,

And we all are the work of Thy hand.

— Isaiah 64:7

PART IV.

GOD AND COUNTRY

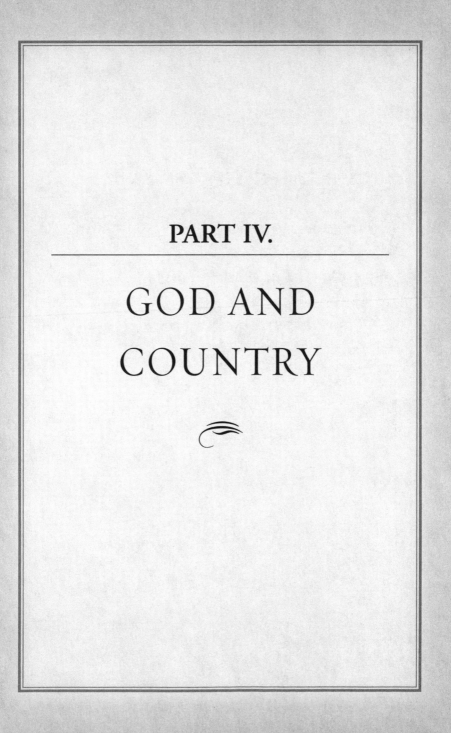

Why would God care about politics?

How does America fit into God's plan?

How did God help build/raise up America?

How has turning away from God led
to national decline?

Halloween Is Bigger
than Christmas

This book is being published between Halloween and Christmas for a specific reason. Halloween is now almost bigger than Christmas in the United States of America. That is a further example of the decline of Western civilization, which was built upon Christianity, not paganism.

My desire in publishing this book now is to somewhat counter the overwhelming influence of the atheists and the agnostics upon our culture.

Across the landscape of America at Halloween, whether it be on suburban lawns or in workplaces, we see little skeletons and cobwebs on lawns, on doors, and even in the workplace. Has anyone noticed that the cross and anything else related to Jesus has been driven out of the workplace? "You can't do that! You can't have anything religious on your desk at work."

But you can hang a skeleton from your workplace cubicle? That tells you the anti-God forces are now dictating the terms of our belief system, to believe in nothing but paganism. This section of the book is my attempt to make people aware of the cultural battle being fought and how it affects the souls of people in our nation and around the world. Because I am sure that if God were more present in our daily lives, whether it be the Ten

Commandments in a classroom, a Jesus statue on your work desk, a Bible proudly displayed in your cubicle, or a prayer session from time to time at work, there would be less drug use and less insanity overall. That is why this book is being published just after the pagan obsession with cobwebs and skeletons at Halloween.

I can hear people saying, "Oh, don't make such a big deal about it. Just celebrate Halloween with all the other white suburbanite fools." Voltaire was an observer of Parisian life and became famous for writing about the foibles of Parisian society. I am not that high up on the totem pole. I write primarily about the foibles of white middle-class suburbanites.

One of the residences I broadcast from is in a white, suburban middle-class community. Don't get me wrong; the residents are nice people. They don't want to offend anybody. Their lawns are clean and clipped; their garbage is put out on the right day; their cans are picked up on the correct day. There's not a leaf left in the driveway because that would be disgraceful. They're nice enough people.

But there's a big "but" attached to that. I've made a certain observation: the larger the number of Halloween displays on a

How is the faithful city

Become a harlot!

She that was full of justice,

Righteousness lodged in her,

But now murderers.

—Isaiah 1:21

Thy silver is become dross,

Thy wine mixed with water.

Thy princes are rebellious,

And companions of thieves;

Every one loveth bribes,

And followeth after rewards;

They judge not the fatherless,

Neither doth the cause of the widow come unto them.

— Isaiah 1:22–23

$\mathfrak{T}$he vile person shall be no more called liberal,

Nor the churl said to be noble.

For the vile person will speak villainy,

And his heart will work iniquity,

To practise ungodliness, and to utter wickedness
against the LORD,

To make empty the soul of the hungry,

And to cause the drink of the thirsty to fail.

— Isaiah 32:5–6

lawn or a house, the more ghosts, the more eerie things that they put up for their children and the neighborhood children, the more liberal the inhabitants are. It's just an observation. I don't have any ghosts hanging from my house. So if you're trying to find my house, it's the one *without* ghosts hanging from the trees and eerie spiderwebs across the hedge.

The American people have given up their religion and their civilization and replaced them with a sort of death worship. I know a lot of people would say, "Come on. It's Halloween. The kids just eat candy corn and have fun."

But it's more than that. It's symbolic. This obscure pagan holiday has become bigger than the July Fourth celebration of independence from Great Britain, bigger than almost any other American holiday, bigger than *any* religious holiday. People who don't go to church, who wouldn't be caught dead in a church, drape fake spiderwebs on their hedges, celebrating what? The day of the dead? These are symptoms of a dying civilization.

The instruments also of the churl are evil;

He deviseth wicked devices

To destroy the poor with lying words,

And the needy when he speaketh right.

But the liberal deviseth liberal things;

And by liberal things shall he stand.

—Isaiah 32:7-8

Burning Man

I never went to the Burning Man festival in my life. Not once. I didn't go to Woodstock. My idea of fun wasn't lying around in the dirt, smoking marijuana or taking LSD. So I didn't go. To me, the Catskill mountains are about clean water and nice leaves, not that.

But every year, I have to look at the paper and read about celebrities and tech execs with luxury camps flocking to Burning Man.

What is the value in going to an event where people walk around stoned out of their minds? Why does anyone go to the desert to an event where everyone gets stoned and drugged, with tattoos on their noses, tattoos on their eyeballs? What is this? Is there something wrong with me because I don't go to an event like this or find it revolting?

What is Burning Man? Idiots in the desert, wearing idiotic costumes while stoned? And what are they doing burning an effigy? If this isn't biblical, I don't know what is. This is what the Bible wrote about.

Burning Man is exactly what the Bible warned us about, the worship of false gods. It's the epitome of paganism. And why do people go to it? Because they don't believe in religion; they don't believe in God. This has replaced it. And they go to have a good time, you might say. But what is the good time about?

They call it a "festival." What is a festival about? This past year, they sold 30,000 tickets in less than thirty-five minutes, according to the *Reno Gazette-Journal*. And then we read about the celebrities who attend. Katy Perry, Paris Hilton, and others were among them.

Paris Hilton is so "yesterday." Of course she'd be at Burning Man. She can't get a job anywhere else; where else would she be? She flew coach into Reno and appeared half naked on a float. And personally, I don't even know who Katy Perry is. I've heard she's a celebrity. And of course, she wouldn't miss Burning Man for the world.

And nowadays you can find Silicon Valley there in force. Do you know how much tickets to this fiasco cost? It's $425 per person plus an $80 vehicle pass.

The classic East Coast liberal thinks anyone who believes in God is crazy, a fantasist, a lunatic, out of touch with reality, etc. Only they know reality because they live in Manhattan or Brooklyn. But if I said to you that Burning Man is directly related to biblical teachings, you'd have to understand that Exodus 24:4 in the original, Jewish Bible, says, "Thou shalt not make unto thee any graven image or any likeness of anything that is in heaven above or that is in the earth beneath or that is in the water under the earth."

They are making wooden effigies and burning them. That's what the Bible warned against. That these are the end of days— that's what people who are religious believe, when you see things like this. So the degenerate cities like San Francisco, where Nancy Pelosi says a leather parade is part of her value system, where men whip each other with whips in public and she calls it wholesome, are the antithesis of biblical teachings.

This is why there is a split in America between those of us who see what this is and those of us who don't see what this is. It is between those of us who say, as George Orwell said, "The more people chant about their freedom and how free they are, the more loudly I hear their chains rattling." That's what I see in San Francisco. The larger the number of nose rings, the more chains I hear rattling. The more they scream about how free they are, the more I know they're enslaved.

And the more I see people flocking to Burning Man, the more I know America is degenerating into the house of bondage. Because that is absolutely an example of bondage. Deuteronomy 32:17 says, "They sacrificed unto demons, no-gods, Gods that they knew not, New gods that came up of late, Which your fathers dreaded not." All of you who are going into the desert, realize where you are going. You are going into Hell itself.

The New Marrano Jews

I want you to understand how so many Americans were shaped by the entertainment business in the 1950s. And then if I jump cut to what the degenerates are doing to your children's minds today, you will see that the Devil the Bible warns us about is very much alive. He's behind every camera in Hollywood. They are all used to pervert your child, to lead your child astray. I'll stand by those words.

When did you last see a movie, other than one produced by a Christian, that told you something other than to follow the path of sex, drugs, and rock and roll? All cops are bad; all minorities are good. All white men are secretly evil. Corporate executives are crooks. Every corporation is thieving. And who is producing these films? Corporations. It's a very sad time in American history.

I'm a great lover of blues music, especially the older blues music, because almost all of it derived from gospel music. All the great music by black people at that time came out of the gospel music tradition. Most of them began in church choirs. Some of the great jazzmen of all time came out of church choirs. You wouldn't know that listening to the media. They don't want you to see the connection between divinity and creativity. But there is a direct connection between divinity and creativity in more artists than you can imagine.

In Hollywood, they have to hide it. There are some great actors around who are true believers, but they'll never show it. They'd never get another job in Hollywood because of the degenerates who run it. If the degenerates floating around on their four-hundred-foot yachts ever knew that some of the greatest actors of our time pray to God or believe in Jesus, those actors would never work in that town again.

So they keep it to themselves like the Marrano Jews in Spain. The Marrano Jews lived during the Inquisition, when the Catholics were killing anyone who didn't follow their way. They were very much like the radical Muslims today. Yes, there is precedent for what the radical Muslims are doing today. Either you believed in what the Catholics believed in, or they killed you. They'd let you convert, but if you didn't, they burned you at the stake or had you drawn and quartered. They were very similar to ISIS.

So the Marranos converted to Christianity outwardly, to avoid being killed. But secretly they practiced their Judaism in the basements of their houses. That is why, to this day, there are many Catholics who look Jewish. You'll find the same thing in Sicily. Why do so many Jews eat Italian food? That's an old joke, but it's because a lot of Italians have Jewish ancestry. It's well known here in San Francisco that different regions of Italy have people with different origins. And there is a region of Italy where the people are very well known for their financial intelligence. Many Genovese Italians descend from Jewish people who converted to Christianity.

A while back, I visited a synagogue in Saint Thomas, in the Virgin Islands. I had heard there was a sand floor, but I didn't know why until I went there. The woman there told me they had sand on the floor to remind them that they couldn't practice their Judaism in Spain, from whence they'd fled. So they put sand on the floor to absorb the sound of their chanting in Hebrew. When I walked onto that sand floor, I was in communion with people who had been oppressed, tortured, or murdered for their beliefs. It made me feel something I hadn't felt before.

So the devoutly religious actors in Hollywood are like the Marrano Jews. They hide their faith to keep their jobs, to keep from being banished from Hollywood society. If they said they believed in God, the degenerates would call them KKK members, Nazis, deplorables, and run them out of town. And of course the good, tolerant liberals would gang up on those Christians.

Run ye to and fro through the streets of Jerusalem,

And see now, and know,

And seek in the broad places thereof,

If ye can find a man,

If there be any that doeth justly, that seeketh truth;

And I will pardon her.

And though they say: 'As the LORD liveth',

Surely they swear falsely.

— Jeremiah 5:1–2

Guilt in Religion—
Hillary's Sins Washed Away

It's a depressing thing, all the guilt. Religion is so full of guilt. You walk around, and it's like everything you do is wrong. You look wrong, you think wrong, your mind does this, your mind does that. You open your mouth, you're wrong; you breathe, you're wrong. That's religion. Original religion was based on guilt.

How that came about, I'll never know. Why did anyone go along with the idea that you're no good no matter what you do? How did anyone ever come to believe this? But it's still there. You suffer for everything you do. You look at someone wrong, your intention is wrong, you're a rebel; that's wrong. You're brusque; that's wrong. You have a confused heart; that's wrong. You must bring a burnt offering because you did this or that.

I burnt my toast this morning. That was my burnt offering.

You committed a sin because you were deceitful, had improper thoughts, used coercion, desecrated. . . . That's why I walked away from religion. I didn't like the guilt. Maybe it works for some people.

You commit a sin in business dealings by eating and drinking? Just by eating and drinking you commit a sin? By taking interest and usury? I don't do that. I don't own a bank. I'm not Wells Fargo. You commit a sin by having a haughty demeanor. Okay, that's all of Hollywood. Commit a sin by the prattle of your lips, by a glance of the eye, with proud looks? Should you walk around like a schmuck? What does that mean, proud looks? Is it a sin to put on a nice outfit? Or are you required to look like a loser?

Casting off the yoke of Heaven with impudence, passing judgment by a begrudging eye are also sins that you're supposed to apologize for.

The word *obduracy* isn't even used in America anymore. No one even knows what the word means. Ask the average welfare recipient what obduracy means. They want to know how much is in it for them. Running to do evil, talebearing, swearing in vain, causeless hatred, embezzlement. Embezzlement? The whole Democratic Party would be out of business if it ever tried to atone for that sin.

Even having a confused heart is a sin. Who doesn't have a confused heart? You're supposed to apologize for all of this? The day I lost my religion, I'm not going to tell you that story. The day I found my religion is another story.

In many ways, the last presidential campaign became semireligious. What is odd is that a woman as corrupt as Hillary Clinton could have been seen as the holier one. That's astounding. She's about as corrupt an individual as you can possibly get in a skirt. But because of people like Anderson Stupor, her sins were suddenly washed away. There was no Arab Spring, no displacement of millions of people in the Middle East because of her policies, no Clinton cash. Nothing. She's cleaner than Trump, purer than him, more moral than him. Can you believe that? How the world turns. And look who made the decision for us: the media gurus of deceit.

How Revolutionaries
Kill God

The fact of the matter is, I'm appealing to liberals out there—real liberals—to understand that liberalism can be a philosophy that's operational and accepting of other people, not a winner-take-all philosophy that crushes anyone who disagrees with them. What's happened now is that there is no true liberalism left in the political world. It seems to have dissolved. I don't know when, and I can't point a finger at who dissolved it.

But the true liberals are gone. You can call them progs, as I do, because it's kind of a descriptive term to describe the progressives today. It has a derogatory tone to it, which it should, because the progs are not leading us forward. They're leading us backward into a Soviet era we will all regret, including the progs themselves, who will also feel the steel of the guillotine, once it starts falling. The French Revolution should have taught us one thing: the guillotine has an endless desire for blood.

I've tried to put politics aside. It's so painful. The bigger the liars, the more they scream for Trump's head. The more they're stealing from the government, the louder they scream for Trump's head. The more they're robbing from the Treasury, the more they call you a deplorable or a KKK or a Nazi. As I said, I'm not a prophet, but I can say with some conviction that I know what I'm talking about regarding the phonies in the media. And I'll say it again: this country is moving back toward God.

Don't expect to see that in a poll. Don't expect to see it on CNN or MSNBC or Fox News. I'm telling you because I have a better stethoscope on America's heartbeat than they do. The country is turning back to faith because there is nowhere else to go. We had faith in Donald Trump, and I'm sorry to say many of us have lost our faith in government itself.

There has been a palace coup. Trump is much like a figurehead now. He says things we want to hear, but then nothing happens. Or worse, the reverse happens a day later.

Many people feel lost and don't know which way to turn. So, many people will go back to church. But then they'll have another problem in their hands. The church they grew up in is not the church they'll go back to today. You take a look at who is on the pulpit in most of these reform temples, most of these liberal churches. They're going to sell you social activism rather than God. That's going to be a battle you're going to have to face on your own.

I don't have that problem because I don't go to houses of worship. I don't like people lecturing me. If I need a ritual, I'll go for the ritual. I'm moved by rituals, whether they be in a church or a synagogue. On Christmas Eve, I like to go to the Grace Cathedral in San Francisco and listen to the service. I was pleasantly surprised last year to see that they didn't infect the service with liberalism. I thought there would be a radical feminist coming out to preach politics, not God. But the service was traditional and moving.

I sat there and felt the vibes of all the good people of this city through the years. And I live it. I pay almost no attention to the inveiglers who have taken over the Church, the papacy, and the synagogues. Let God be the judge of all of that, not me. I'm one man wandering on this lonely planet of ours, trying to find his way.

Wherefore should I pardon thee?

The children have forsaken Me,

And sworn by no-gods;

And when I had fed them to the full,
they committed adultery,

And assembled themselves in troops
at the harlots' houses.

— Jeremiah 5:7

An Unlikely Choice

Many people believe that Trump winning this election, by hook or by crook, had God's hand involved in it. Does that mean Trump is a prophet? No, but God saved America at the last minute. He saved us as sure as I am sitting here from this bunch of atheistic anti-American vermin who have tried to destroy us from within.

Sometimes God chooses odd people to do His bidding. Look at the story of His choosing Moses. He said, "Moses, I'm choosing you. You're the chosen one to lead your people." Moses replied, "Oh, come on, don't pick on me. I don't want to do this. I can't do it. I stutter. I'm not good looking. I have a bad face. My skin is no good. No, pick someone else." God said, "That's why I'm choosing you, because you are imperfect."

When you consider that and then you look within yourself, you realize that you also can be chosen for things on this earth. No matter how humble you may be, you could be chosen to do something great. You may have already experienced that.

You see, the people who are chosen by God or by fate or by destiny to do wonderful things often don't even know they've been chosen to do them. I've told these stories before, and they resonate in me at times.

But I truly believe that America can be saved. I think we're seeing only the beginning of the salvation. I believe that once the rats are forced out of the White House, once the rats are purged from the media, it will be clearer. Make no mistake about it, the vermin behind the rats that you see in the media, they're businessmen and businesswomen at the end of the day. If they see that because of the left-wing fanaticism their listenership or viewership has collapsed, they're going to start reaching out to people on the other side, the 51 percent of Americans they've spat on for the last ten years. They've been spitting on you. They said you're nobody, you're nothing. You don't go to the movies, you don't watch television. You don't buy books, you don't read this, you don't read that.

But they've found out that you exist. At some point the boards of directors of the media giants are going to begin talking to you with respect. And then voices like mine will be heard across the land. You will start to hear voices like mine. They will start appearing in the most unexpected outlets you could ever imagine. The only reason is that the rats behind the scenes are businesspeople and all they look at is the bottom line.

They've finally awakened to the fact that they were spitting on 51 percent of America. Laughing at you, mocking you, calling you every name under the sun—the deplorables, the despicables, the rubes, the breeders. But you are the backbone of America, and you have only just begun.

You know, I keep hearing that immigrants are the backbone of America. I keep hearing that they do the jobs that Americans won't do. Then why are we bringing in fifteen-year-old girls with babies? Why are we bringing in Muslims with six children? Why is it that the immigrants have a much higher use of the welfare system than do the natives of this country? If you can answer

They are become as well-fed horses, lusty stallions;

Every one neigheth after his neighbour's wife.

Shall I not punish for these things?

Saith the LORD;

And shall not My soul be avenged

On such a nation as this?

— Jeremiah 5:8–9

those questions, you'll come to understand that virtual criminals have been running the nation.

And they're not just ordinary criminals who are doing it for personal gain, although there is a tremendous amount of personal gain in flooding the country with immigrants. Catholic Charities USA ripped $2.5 billion out of the tax base last year. Lutheran Family Services is another one. They are criminal organizations, in my opinion. Do you think that because the word "Catholic" is in front of the name, it can't be run by a bunch of thieves? I suggest you look at the directors' salaries. Ask yourself, "Why are we spending more than two billion dollars on Catholic Charities? And what have they given us?"

Oh, wait a minute, I remember what they gave us. Why that young fellow last year in Ohio, he was brought in with his five Muslim brethren from Somalia. Oh, yeah, it was Catholic Charities that put him in Columbus, Ohio. Then why hasn't Catholic Charities been sued by the victims he ran over and knifed? The answer is that I'm not a lawyer.

Let's return to Exodus in the Bible. If you can put the Jewish part aside for one minute, just listen to this. This is God speaking. He says, "Moreover, you shall provide out of all the people, able men such as fear God, men of truth, hating unjust gain, and place such over them to be rulers of thousands, rulers of hundreds, rulers of fifties and rulers of tens." That's a beautiful statement. Able men such as fear God, men of truth hating unjust gain.

Isn't that what we want in a leader? Isn't that what we prayed for, that we'd get rid of the deceit in the White House? Do you say Obama's not corrupt? He didn't self-gain, did he? He received a $60 million book advance soon after leaving office! And flew on private jets and enjoyed vacations on megayachts owned by the very "millionaires and billionaires" he so often condemned while in office.

You may say that's petty compared to the rest of federal spending. I understand that. But what about the unjust gain of steering contracts to all the people in the gangster solar panel business who have provided very low wattage for a very high price? How's that for corruption?

Now, do I think that it's going to end under Trump? Absolutely not. I think it may get worse. If the RNC gets its hands on the government again, and it looks as though they did, they're going to roll in the gold like pigs roll in you-know-what. We know what the Republican machine is like. They're like pigs in mud.

ᘓᤱᣢᣣ

Your land, strangers devour it

in your presence,

—Isaiah 1:7

ᘒᤱᤲᣢᘔ

For of old time I have broken thy yoke,

And burst thy bands,

And thou saidst: 'I will not transgress';

Upon every high hill

And under every leafy tree

Thou didst recline, playing the harlot.

— Jeremiah 2:20

Faith and Freedom

I had a caller on *The Savage Nation* who compared me to an Old Testament prophet warning people about the dangers of liberalism. It was just after I had done a show segment on the wonderful movie *Hacksaw Ridge*. The hero, Desmond Doss, drew courage from the Bible and eventually earned the Congressional Medal of Honor without firing a shot. But the caller's point was that everything I had done up to my book *Scorched Earth* was like an Old Testament prophet, while with *Trump's War* I played the role of John the Baptist, who said, "He must become greater, while I decrease." He was referring to the many times I'd had Donald Trump on my show, introducing the man who would bring my message of borders, language, and culture to an even wider audience than I already had. It was a very interesting insight.

As I said at the beginning of this book, God does not do the heavy lifting for us. It is up to us to find our connection to God and to do His will here. I truly believe that my lifelong fight for our borders, language, and culture is part of my mission. As I've said many times, it's indisputable that I helped Trump get elected. It's equally indisputable that, as imperfect as he is, he represented the only chance to restore a free, just, and godly nation given the crossroads we were at last November.

But what is my role now that Trump has been elected? That same caller suggested that winning the election was akin to the ancient Israelites being freed from bondage in Egypt. That's not a bad analogy, but let's not forget that even the Israelites didn't go directly from Egypt to the Promised Land. Not only did they have to wander for forty years in the desert before reaching Canaan, they had to conquer the Promised Land before taking possession of it.

That forty years of wandering wasn't just bad luck. In Exodus, God makes the Israelites wander in the desert because of their infidelity to Him and their decisions to do evil in His sight.

What a great metaphor for where we are today. Yes, we won a crucial election that may have saved our country from irreparable ruin. But Trump hasn't been perfect. He's already taken many wrong turns, as when he allowed the neocons to manipulate him into bombing Syria, based on hearsay evidence of Assad gassing his own people. But, like Moses, who also disobeyed God's will while leading the Israelites to Canaan, he is still leading America toward its own Promised Land. He's made mistakes along the way and will likely make many more in the future, but at least he's taking us in the right direction.

Let's not forget that we've had great victories along the way as well, just as the Israelites did at Ai and Jericho. Trump has succeeded in stemming the tide of unvetted refugees from nations with high numbers of Islamic terrorists. He had to take that one all the way to the Supreme Court. And he's been able to get rid of the most onerous regulations Obama put on businesses, particularly in the fossil fuel industries. I remain cautiously optimistic that he won't let the sellouts in his party go too far in repealing environmental regulations, under the pretense of reversing Obama's, which were far too restrictive.

Most important, Trump has legalized patriotism again. Though he has personally had to endure withering attacks from the media thought police, he has exposed them for the frauds they are to large portions of the population who never suspected just how much "fake news" they were being subjected to.

As for me, I'm always asking myself what's ahead and where I should go. To be honest, I don't have an answer to that right now. I feel that I've done my job. Some mornings, I wake up and feel like a salmon that has swum upstream. I feel I have done the biggest thing I could possibly do in my life and there's nothing left to do. But then I remember Moses, who spent the rest of his life trying to get his people to the Promised Land *after* he had freed them from bondage in Egypt. And I know there is still a lot of work to be done to save our nation.

Let's not forget, winning elections has yielded disappointing results before. We thought we had accomplished something when we sent conservatives to Washington in three straight elections, from 2010 to 2014. And what happened? We were stabbed in the back by John Boehner and Mitch McConnell. Boehner may be gone, but McConnell is still there, along with a bunch of other RINOs and sellouts.

They have done it to us before, and I don't want them to be allowed to do it again. If I must again be the only one out there willing to stand up and take the chance of having the Donald Trump camp reject me, cast me out from Eden, I must live with that. So if I'm going to live in Nod, I'll live in Nod. I've lived here my whole life. I'll stay here. I didn't expect to be invited into the Garden of Eden for supporting Donald Trump. And if I'm cast out because I dare criticize the president and the RNC, so be it. I've wandered in the desert; I'll continue to wander in the desert. It's that simple.

I'm the one conservative who hasn't forgotten *why* we sent Donald Trump to Washington. It's not enough simply to have him in the White House, throwing tweet-bombs at the media. We sent him there to restore our borders, language, and culture. We need the wall built, the military restored, the economy repaired with fair trade deals that put America first, and ISIS destroyed.

We've sent congressmen to Washington for six years trying to make a difference, and the swamp dwellers in Washington have stabbed them in the back and spat in our faces. I don't want them to do it to us again and think they can get away with it because we're not going to do anything about it. There are millions of us who will do something.

That's what I want everyone to understand. Our battle is just beginning. Thank God Trump took Mattis out of retirement. He's going to really scare hell out of you-know-who. The liberals are going to run like rats off a ship out of the military. Maybe he'll reappoint all the people in the military Obama purged in Stalinist fashion. But even Mattis has a lot of work ahead of him.

It all comes down to us. We the people must support Trump when he tries to do the things we sent him to Washington to do. I had another caller who told me he had prayed for Trump to win the election. He said, "When Obama got elected I was very confused, because I pray all the time. I'm a Christian. And I realized the Bible teaches that all work together for the good, for those that love the Lord. I realized that Obama and the Left gave us Donald Trump. When the American people seen how vile and nasty these people really are, they come in droves to vote and support Donald Trump. And the churches were filling up bigger than I'd seen in thirty years."

That caller said even more than he realized. Yes, it may have been God's will that Trump won the election, but God didn't vote

> **I** will even gather you from the peoples, and assemble
> you out of the countries where ye have been scattered,
> and I will give you the land of Israel.
>
> —Ezekial 11:17

for us. He didn't reach into the minds of people about to vote for Hillary and zap their minds to change them into Trump voters. Neither did the Russians, by the way. No, the people had to make that decision themselves. They had to decide to vote for Trump and go back to church themselves.

God gave us everything we need to do the right thing. He gave us the ability to reason. He gave us dominion over an entire planet. He gave us an innate sense of right and wrong. But He's not going to wave His hand and make everything right after we here on Earth have screwed it up. We're going to have to do it ourselves.

For my part, I'm going to continue to do what I have done for three decades. I'm going to keep giving you my analysis of the latest news. I'm going to use my large platform to let Donald Trump know we're with him against the forces of evil, that we support his fight to take America back. And I'm going to speak up when he strays from the path, as I did when he bombed Syria or when he allowed his Twitter feuds to get his presidency off track. A true supporter lets you know when you've strayed off course. I'm a true supporter of Trump and his message, because it was my message before it was Trump's.

Besides, what did I expect for having backed Trump? I didn't expect anything. I didn't want a job. Nor do I want one now. I can't work in a bureaucracy. I'm not moving anywhere. This is what I'm meant to do, which is to broadcast and write books. So the umbrella I bought to take to the inauguration will be auctioned off on eBay one day. It did not go to the inauguration, and I don't expect it to go to future State of the Union addresses, either. I will auction it off and give the money to a charity for veterans. It'll probably bring in a lot of money.

There is one thing I would like to get out of all of this: maybe one day Donald Trump will try to persuade the British government to take my name off the UK banned list. I'm still legally banned from visiting that country, basically for telling the truth. That's one thing I hope to get out of all this work I'm doing trying to restore some semblance of Western civilization. But it's not what's most important to me, in the end. Moses never made it into the Promised Land, but he knew his people were going to make it. I can certainly forgo making it into the United Kingdom if I can leave knowing my people are going to achieve their Promised Land after I move on.

The Meaning of Passover

I talked about Exodus in an earlier chapter, but I would like to explain the meaning of the Passover holiday in this one. I'm talking about what it means to a person beyond the ritual and how it can be used to improve oneself. Again, if a religion doesn't in some way give you courage, strength, or hope, that religion is useless as far as I'm concerned.

Religion should give you some connection to the ultimate power that drives the universe. I have studied a variety of religions during my life, at some times more actively than at others. I've looked for the truth in so many places and in so many ways that my heads spins just thinking about it. It has all been an attempt to find meaning in life: What am I doing here? What's the purpose of life? Why do good people suffer? Why do bad people sometimes not suffer? These are the eternal questions. If you find answers in religion, you're lucky. Most people don't.

Most people, in my experience, sit in church or synagogue, go along with the program, and don't even know what they're doing. They hear nothing. They're numb. They go in numb, and they come out numb. They take away nothing from it. Occasionally a person is touched or reached by one of the holy books sitting there or by a teacher. Occasionally someone is touched, and that's good enough. You can't expect an entire flock to be touched.

But there is a higher thing in religion, whether it be Judaism, Christianity, Buddhism, Islam, or even Hinduism. All of it is an attempt to tap into some power. Even paganism, although not one of the five major religions, is people trying to tap into a power that runs through them. They want the power. They want the energy. They want to be innervated. They want to feel the power. They don't want to be denervated. They don't want to go to a church and come away feeling weaker than when they went in.

Every year people flock to Lourdes in France by the hundreds of thousands. They believe that if they touch the holy water in the grotto at the Sanctuary of Our Lady of Lourdes, they will be healed. They believe it can make the crippled walk, the blind see, the deaf hear. Sometimes people will jump up and say, "I'm healed! I'm healed!"

What are they going there for? They're going there for a "miracle." What's a miracle? It's the energy, the power that drives the entire universe. It's the energy that makes a blade of grass start from a seed, a dormant, dead thing, and turn into a beautiful green thing.

That seed is you. Many of us are walking around like a husk, a dead seed. But inside the apparently dead seed, there is a living, green piece of grass, just as inside an acorn, there's a great tree. Many of us remain a seed, live our whole life as a seed, waiting for someone, whether it be a woman for a man or vice versa. We wait for someone or something to awaken the seed into life and make it come alive, make a piece of green grass or a tree grow from it.

People often try to find that through religion. Some do. Some go to church every Sunday. Some go every day. A Sunni Muslim prays five times a day. He believes he's reaching God five times a day; he feels the energy. Many of us cannot feel it at all when we're alone, but when we go into a temple, a mosque, a church, we can.

Have you ever been in St. Patrick's Cathedral in New York City on Christmas Eve? If you have, or if you have been in an Orthodox Jewish temple in Brooklyn, New York, when there are five thousand men chanting at the same time, or even in a village setting where there are twenty men chanting, you've felt an energy that you will never feel alone. So there is an argument for the congregation. But I haven't touched on Passover yet.

The Jewish people are a very small minority numerically, both in the world and in the United States of America. I think even nonreligious Jews have a seder. Now, many Christians understand what a seder is. Sometimes Christians go to seders because they have Jewish friends or someone in their family has married a Jewish person. It's a rather peaceful, nice, long meal with various ritualistic events, including the unleavened bread, or matzoh.

The unleavened bread signifies the time of haste when the Jewish people were fleeing Egypt and had to make bread in the desert. They didn't have time to allow the dough to rise. The children love this kind of thing if they understand it at all. I don't know if they even teach it to the children anymore. The children understand that their ancestors were once slaves, but they don't really know what that means.

A modern Passover seder may not mean the same thing to people today as the ancient one did to the Israelites. I'm not against tradition, I'm just saying a lot of people don't hear the message anymore or want to listen. Although they may say, "Our ancestors were slaves," it has no meaning.

What it can mean for us today is that we are still slaves in our own life and we can break the bonds of slavery any time we want. If you take it as a personal seder, a personal Passover, you can learn to release yourself from your own chains. Whether they be alcohol, drugs, sexual addiction, gambling addiction, you could say you are a slave. You could come to understand you are enslaved. You can decide, from that day forward, to seek to break those chains of bondage and become a free man or a free woman. That's another way to interpret the significance of Passover, to give it a modern meaning, an eternal meaning. You must take meaning from the ancient and give it some modern meaning or else it loses its value altogether.

To most people it has to do with chicken, chopped liver, fish, brisket, and things of that nature. It's about drinking too much wine, because you're supposed to drink four cups of wine. For too many people, it's an excuse to get drunk around a communal table in a nice setting with a clean tablecloth and good silverware. But the Passover Seder is about breaking our bondage.

𝕱or though thy people, O Israel,
be as the sand of the sea,

Only a remnant of them shall return;

An extermination is determined, overflowing
with righteousness.

—Isaiah 10:22

Buddhism: The Religion of Submission

What ties together everything in the Jewish scriptures is the responsibility for man to actively seek God and do His will. That's where I believe the Judeo-Christian tradition is superior to Buddhism. Whereas Jews and Christians are called by their scriptures and belief systems to actively change their own lives and try to make the world a better place, Buddhism is very much a religion of submission and accepting the world as it is.

I remember a caller on *The Savage Nation* who had a wonderful insight into this. He said, "Well, I respect the Buddhist perspective. I understand the desire to remove oneself from the karmic wheel. But it has always struck me, in a sense, as being a dichotomy, in that the other side of that coin is an avoidance of the human experience. You have no attachment; you seek no goals. In essence, you seek to become an empty cup."

I couldn't have agreed more with that caller. When I was much younger and doing a lot of reading on the subject, I concluded myself that all religions are somewhat specific to the nation and the people at the place and time in which they were established. Buddhism was a religion that was very good for people who were serfs and had no chance to advance themselves. No matter what they did, no matter how they did it, they could never move ahead.

So they naturally embraced a religion that teaches that it's the norm to get nowhere; that no matter what you do, you're going to struggle and fail. That was their situation under the sociopolitical system they lived under, and they developed a religion that would allow them to cope with or make sense of their lot in life under that system. So Buddhism was ultimately a religion for submission to the inevitable of getting nowhere in life.

It's like all religions that appeal to people who are broken and suffering in this life, because they promise eternal life in another place. That's fine and good to believe in. It can be very healthy and keep you going and make you a noble person.

No Man Is an Island

How many of you know that "for whom the bell tolls" comes from a great poem, which approaches a religious piece, by the great dead white male poet John Donne? It's a short one. He was writing something called Devotions Upon Emergence Occasions and said, "No man is an island, entire of itself; every man is a piece of the continent, a part of the main." He meant that although we're individuals, we're also part of a whole, which makes living as individuals possible. The death of any one person diminishes the life of every other, because it diminishes the whole. That's why his famous ending says, "never send to know for whom the bell tolls; it tolls for thee." It is no longer taught by the polyps in the US academic establishment, the polyps who have turned academia into a cauldron of left-wing hatred for everything Caucasian, everything European, everything that is great on this earth, created by whites but now expunged by the polyps who have taken over every aspect of the academy.

What does that have to do with Trump? Nothing, in a way. But the poem begins with, "No man is an island." Trump isn't an island. And as Chuck Schumer and the other *illegitimi* on the left continue to tear him apart, they do not realize they're tearing themselves apart. As they tear apart the truth, as they tear apart decency, as they tear apart democracy, as they tear apart the presidency, they're washing away our nation. And if you think they're attacking only Trump, you are mistaken. They're attacking the foundations of our nation.

I've shared this great meditation because it's as good as anything that the ancients wrote. But there is an ancient one-line passage from *Ethics of the Fathers* that says, "Do not judge alone, for none can judge alone except one," meaning only God can judge alone. Apparently, Chuck Schumer forgot all of that after he put down his religious studies, if he ever had any. And after tearing apart Donald Trump on completely fallacious grounds, the polyps in the Democrat Party live for one thing only, and that is to destroy. To destroy, destroy, destroy.

But here's the odd part: instead of facing the real enemy of Western civilization, radical Islam, they have created a false enemy called Russia. Suddenly, Russia is the big enemy. What has Russia done to harm the United States? The answer is absolutely nothing. In fact, were it not for Russian jets, ISIS would still be cutting off heads and setting people on fire alive. It was the Russian air force under Vladimir Putin that started to destroy ISIS, not Barry Hussein Obama, who refused to do the job.

Civilization itself is under attack right now. Not long ago, I received an e-mail from a very famous Democrat attorney. I'm talking about an old-line, JFK-era Democrat. Don't confuse people like him with the so-called progressives of today. I'm talking about an old-time, fair-minded liberal. There were such men at one time. They practically don't exist anymore. This attorney wrote me an impassioned e-mail about how Donald Trump should handle the James Comey scandal.

He said there's only one way for him to handle it, and "Of course I told the FBI director 'if you can.' I didn't say 'you should.' *If you can*, drop this, because he's a good man. Flynn is a good man. He's my friend."

That shows loyalty. Do you understand? That shows Donald Trump has something none of the Democrat polyps have: integrity and loyalty to friends. Do you understand what's going on here? Loyalty, integrity, things Schumer never learned in the dirty streets of Brooklyn. Things Nancy Pelosi apparently never learned.

The attorney added, "There's nothing illegal with that." He gave me some other advice: There's absolutely no case whatsoever for impeachment. None. In fact, if you think there is, you're really living in a dream world.

I received a letter from my attorney, Daniel Horowitz. He said:

Impeachment based upon the Comey memo is very unlikely. Here's why. If Comey really was solicited in a way that was clearly illegal, he had two choices. One, he could submit a report to the Attorney General and seek a prosecution. Two, he could create a memo report and do further investigation. That is, set up a sting or attempt to garner more proof than just his word against the president's. As far as I know, neither took place. A cynic would say that Comey was holding it over Trump as blackmail, but I give no credence to that at all. The power would fade over time, and the delay in reporting would make the use of the threat a bluff. That leaves us with the idea that Comey probably felt pressured, but also believed that the conduct did not constitute a crime. It is the only logical conclusion. Comey is a lawyer and an experienced law enforcement officer. And he is smart and not afraid of anyone as far as I can tell. For these reasons, his noting of the contact but his taking no further action screams to me there is nothing here.

Unfortunately, the propaganda damage has already been done. I received several e-mails from a friend of mine in Los Angeles. He said that in every restaurant he went into, all anyone was talking about, was Trump, Russia, Trump, Russia, Trump, Russia. He said wherever he went, the psychotic liberals had bought it hook, line, and sinker. The idiots in west Hollywood, who don't know their toenails from their DNA, were talking not about the radical Islamic threat to our civilization but about Trump and Russia. So the damage has already been done.

But Trump is doing his work. While under constant assault from the lowest forms of humanity, he continues to do the job we sent him to Washington to do. And if you think I'm going to abandon him like all the Never-Trumpers, stab him in the back and jump ship because all the others are doing it, you're wrong. I'm made of better stuff than that.

I'm not going to join the chorus who are for Ted Cruz or any of the other lessers who could not win. They're now sticking a knife in Trump's back because he's in trouble. The answer should be to stick a knife in the other party's back, not in Trump's. I've said this before, and I will say it again: what is missing is Roy Cohn.

If I were Donald Trump, I would hire a hundred aggressive lawyers under a Roy Cohn–like lawyer and I would investigate all of those who are persecuting me with false charges. I would put ten investigators on every senator, every congressman, every reporter who has it in for me. And once I turned over every rock in their lives and exposed what's real about their own crimes and misdemeanors, you would see most of the persecution cease.

It's astonishing to me how successful propaganda can be. It's shocking to me how the media can take a man like Donald Trump, as flawed as he is, and turn him into a villain. Flawed he is; a villain he is not.

By attacking Trump, what they're really doing is attacking the Americans who voted for him. Make no mistake about it, by attacking Trump they're saying, "Drop dead on the border with

That saith: 'I will build me a wide house

And spacious chambers',

And cutteth him out windows,

And it is ceiled with cedar, and painted with vermilion.

Shalt thou reign, because thou strivest to excel in cedar?

Did not thy father eat and drink, and do justice
and righteousness?

Then it was well with him.

—Jeremiah 22:14–15

Mexico. We love the drugs. We love the crime. We love the illegal aliens. We love the meth dealers pouring over the border. We love the throat cutters with tattoos. We want more of them in our cities because we love the drug trade."

By attacking Trump they're saying, "We love an unfair trade deal where Eddie loses his job. We love jobs going to Canada. We love jobs going to Mexico. We love jobs going to China. We want the white male suffering with nothing in this country. We want the white male out of work. We want him humiliated and broken."

And what are they saying about our language? "We don't want a language in this country. We want a bastardization. We want no one to understand the next man. We want a Tower of Babel."

They are attacking us. They are attacking the core of the nation. They're attacking every last one of us who voted for Trump. Make no mistake about it. The battle lines are drawn. The game has begun. And Michael Savage is not jumping ship just because you think it is convenient for him to do so. I am a loyal man.

It should be noted that both Andrew McCabe and the former director of national intelligence James Clapper, who never shuts his claptrap mouth, have already refuted the Democrats' conspiracy theory. There is absolutely no collusion whatsoever with Russia.

Having said that, my big, high, powerful Democrat lawyer friend said to me, "Trump should give a national press conference. He should have done it already and stopped tweeting." I agree. Trump should stop with the juvenile, adolescent tweeting. It's not presidential. He should give a national press conference in the Oval Office with the Great Seal of the United States in front of him and say, "Yes, I defended General Flynn, because he is a good man. And I would do it again. And number two, yes, I did tell the ambassador about the dangers of radical Islam and its agents' attempts to use laptops to blow up airplanes, because that is my job as president: to protect people. And I would do it again with any other world leader who is our ally." That would be the end of it.

By attacking Donald Trump, the Democrats, neocons, and RINOs are attacking every one of us who voted for him. They're using tactics the Soviet Communists developed in the 1920s and '30s. And what they are doing to Trump they are doing to every one of us, every decent American like you, like me, who went to the polls.

We didn't beat anybody up. We didn't burn anything down. We didn't attack any police. We didn't use the vile tactics of Black Lives Matter or Antifa, a revolutionary communist terrorist group. We don't use the cowardly tactics of those with masks over their faces. We bit our tongues, went to the polls, and voted. By attacking Trump, they are attacking our votes. That means they're attacking democracy.

We all know there's nothing there. We know this whole thing was a creation of the Hillary Clinton campaign, which has snow-balled into a fake-news avalanche they are starting to believe themselves. We must stay strong in this avalanche and not yield to our liberal neighbors. Don't let them run you down. *Illegitimi non carborundum.*

~❦~

Woe unto him that buildeth his house by unrighteousness,
And his chambers by injustice;

That useth his neighbour's service without wages,
And giveth him not his hire;

—Jeremiah 22:13

PART V.

GOD AND MAN

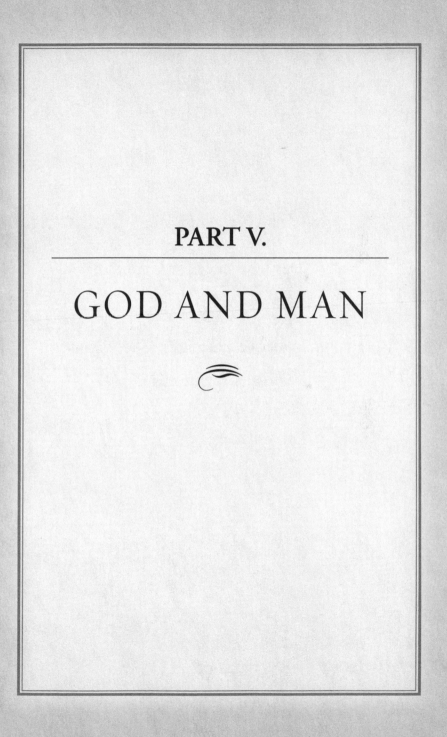

How does God guide your life?

*How does searching for God help
direct your life?*

*How much does God do versus how much
does the individual do?*

Lonesome Boy on Cold Sand

Picture a boy about eleven years old, thin, small, walking alone aimlessly on a cold beach in the middle of the winter in Rockaway, New York. No one is around. The boardwalk is empty. The hotels are silent. What is the boy doing wandering, almost like a bumblebee who'd been sprayed with Raid in the sand?

I was that boy. You see, inside one of the hotels on that wintry day, there was a father-and-son Boy Scout dinner. It was on a Sunday, I believe, and I had attended it. But my father worked seven days a week in his little store, trying to put bread on the table, pay the rent, pay the car bills. So he wasn't with me. I was always alone. I had no father in that regard. He had to work, and I understood that. But it seemed to me that all the other boys had fathers with them and they were happy.

❧

In sitting still and rest shall ye be saved,

In quietness and in confidence shall be your strength;

—Isaiah 30:15

❧

It suddenly dawned on me in the middle of that dinner that I had no father, at least not when I needed him. I still remember almost running out of that room on my own and disappearing onto the sand, the cold sand, and walking by myself. I didn't know where I was going. I don't think I was going to walk into the ocean to kill myself, but I really don't know for sure. I don't know what was in the mind of that eleven-year-old boy.

But I do know that out of nowhere there came the scout leader and a few other men looking for me. I turned around, and there were these kind men. There was Mr. Aaronson. He didn't yell at me. He didn't scream and demand, "What are you doing?" as my father would've done. He was kind, and he reached out to me and took me in his arm. Then, he took me back into the dinner, and I felt that I had just been protected. In many ways, the story is a great metaphor for those of us who are wandering like lost insects, seeking our father or, more important, our Father in Heaven.

The Lord GOD hath given me

The tongue of them that are taught,

That I should know how to sustain with
words him that is weary;

He wakeneth morning by morning,

He wakeneth mine ear

To hear as they that are taught.

— Isaiah 50:4

Five Out of Seven

God is not an equivocator. God doesn't sit on the fence. I've led my life that way. Have I always been up to the standards? I have not. I'm a man. I'm an imperfect creature who doesn't hold himself up above the average person. I am the average person. I try my best, but I often fall back to earth. It's all I can do. I try.

It's like saying I'm going to do push-ups every night. I'd say that five out of seven nights, I do the push-ups, but two nights out of the seven, I don't. I say, "I don't have the strength. I don't want to do it. I just want to go to sleep." It's the same with everything else. Five out of seven times, I do the right thing; two out of seven, I don't.

Jewish Gangster Finds God

I suppose everyone's challenges are relative. I had some hardship in my life, with a father who couldn't be there for me as much as I wanted and with the loss of my brother, Jerome. But there was much joy and love in my childhood as well. My father worked all those hours to provide the kind of opportunities for me that he hadn't had. And I made more good decisions than bad.

One of the more interesting interviews I've done on *The Savage Nation* was with a man who'd grown up under much different circumstances and, for a long time, made much worse decisions than I did. His name is Michael Hardy, and he was the last of the old-time Jewish gangsters. Bugsy Siegel was his godfather. He was, by his own admission, a murderer.

This was a man who grew up in the even tougher Brownsville section of Brooklyn, New York. Growing up in a place like that makes you a hard person. It's inescapable. But there's a difference between being very hard-minded, very tough, very uncompromising, and then crossing that line and being able to cut someone's throat with a soda bottle. I asked him what had driven him to become the criminal he used to be.

He said, "Well, I watched people—I watched these cops come to my mother's house and give envelopes—envelopes all the time. And city councilmen in New York City and Brooklyn, the president came one time. These are all thieves. You understand? That's how I grew up. I watched that, and I understand. Let me tell you the difference between tough and hard. You can get tough sleeping in the street for three weeks. That'll toughen you up. But hard, brother? I've got twenty-seven years in the worst prisons in this country. I'm hard."

I recognized the second part of that answer as somewhat circular. He was saying that prison had made him a hardened criminal but he had been in prison because he was already a criminal. But take note of the first part of his answer: what had started him down the road to a life of crime was his observation of depraved, corrupt local government.

What have I said so many times about the effect our national government has had upon the population? With the Marxist we had in the White House unapologetically lying to the people about Obamacare, running guns to Mexico, targeting political opponents through the IRS, getting caught spying on innocent Americans after his director of national intelligence said he wasn't, and, worst of all, openly condoning rioting in the streets and racial hatred, calling it "protest," the people naturally lost respect for basic decency and law and order. It's very analogous to how Michael Hardy reacted on a local level.

It has biblical precedents as well. Throughout Kings and Chronicles, the fate of the Jewish people is determined by whether they and their leaders were faithful to God. Some kings of Israel and Judah were faithful; others were not. The kings who "built up the high places," meaning temples to gods other than Yahweh, led their people astray. Ultimately, the Jewish people lost the

Promised Land because they followed bad leaders in turning their backs upon God.

I'm not excusing an individual's decision to become a criminal or blaming it on "society," as some do. But leadership does influence the culture, which translates right down to the individual. With strong moral leadership and a culture devoted to God and mutual respect among men, you will have a lot less people making the choices Hardy did.

There is still the nature-versus-nurture question. A lot of people who grew up in Brownsville did not become gangsters. Is the tendency toward crime born in people, rather than something they learn? Because one's brother could have wound up a surgeon, for example, instead of a gangster, even though both grew up in the same rough neighborhood.

Everyone knows stories like this. How many stories my mother used to tell me, because we'd argue over this. She'd ask me, "How do you explain, then, in the same apartment," in the same Lower East Side that she was in, "one brother would be a cop and the other would be a criminal? How did that happen? The same parents, the same background." We'd argue over nature versus nurture. I asked Hardy if he thought he had been born a hard man.

He replied, "Let me answer that question. Kings and killers are born, they're not made. Great kings are made, okay, great, because they step off their throne and they look in people's eyes. They don't look at the top of their heads. But killers are made. Now, I—you want to know the point, the validity of this question, uh, of what I'm saying? I'll tell you what. Six million Jews went into the gas chamber. Six million. Apparently, they, some of them, were hoodwinked, but none of them took the opportunity to kill the last Nazi before they walked into that gas chamber. Just grab a pistol and kill them, knowing you were going to die anyway.

"You understand? I got in a gunfight in, uh, in, um, Holly-wood, this famous gunfight—gunfight at a producer's studio, 1978. Well, I got shot. I got shot six times by this guy, a movie producer. We shot it out right in front. People thought we were making a movie. I was looking out of the corner of my eye while I'm getting nine millimeters pumped into me. Okay? And the last bullet that I—that came out of my gun, I ran and I started beating this guy over the head. I had—I was—I was hit in my jugular vein. I was dying. Okay? That's the difference. If I'm gonna die, I'm gonna take somebody with me."

So are killers born or made? Michael Hardy says both. I must accept the answer he gave me, as far as his opinion is concerned. But it doesn't really matter whether it was nature or nurture; even a killer like Michael Hardy could change. He could have decided not to be a killer any longer. It took a personal decision on his part to become a different person for him to be saved. In other words, by turning to God, he saved himself.

Here is how he put it to me. "Now, what changed my life? I was in Corcoran. Okay, I had sepsis of the spine. Okay, I helped a guy escape out of Donovan Prison, uh, a guy named (Dave Finney). I got the warden fired. I did it for that reason, to get the warden fired. Anyway, what happened is I was dying, okay, and I made a prayer. I said, 'Lord'—this cop came in and he started making me sit up. I had sepsis. I had such pain in my— in my back. I had a few days to go. I said, 'If you ever did this to me on the yard, I'd kill ya. But now I'm dying, so you're coming in here to feed off me.' He said, 'Well.' I said, 'But I'm getting out in a few days.' He said, 'No, you're not, you're doin' life.' I said, 'No, I get out November twenty-seventh.'

He must've looked at the computer—I never seen him again. I was dying. Okay? I made a prayer that night, 'God, please don't let me die. *I promise on my soul I will change my life.'* This is after twenty-seven years of prison—now I finally broke, just a couple of days after I'd finished seventeen years for murder. Okay? I broke. But I only broke—I—but I said, 'I won't take any vengeance on nobody, and I won't do anything except—'"

I had to interrupt him at that point and ask, "Oh, whoa, whoa, whoa. You said you broke? What do you mean, you broke? You changed?"

ꙨꙨ

How canst thou say: 'I am not defiled,

I have not gone after the Baalim'?

See thy way in the Valley,

Know what thou hast done;

—Jeremiah 2:23

ꙨꙨ

"I broke, yes, I did," he replied. "God broke me. God. Adonai. El. He's the one that broke me. He broke me."

It's an interesting use of the word "broke." Hardy said God broke him. I asked him what he meant.

He said, "Because God comes to you. If you—He sends people to you. If you don't listen to Him, okay, He's gonna find a way to break you. He's gonna bring you to Him. And be thankful He does, 'cause if He doesn't, then you're lost. You go into Gehenna, and I know that. This—this is the culture that I come from. This is the Jewish culture. Okay.

W oe to them that devise iniquity

And work evil upon their beds!

When the morning is light, they execute it,

Because it is in the power of their hand.

And they covet fields, and seize them;

And houses, and take them away;

—Micah 2:1–2

"Let me tell you, Michael, I was born into a war zone in Brownsville. Okay? It started out with the, uh, Profaci-Gallo war. Well, I started out with gang wars when I was a kid, um, in Brooklyn on Dead Man's Hill on Crown Heights. Okay, that's where I started out. I went to a school where the principal jumped off the roof. We went to see *Blackboard Jungle*, and we—I thought it was a musical comedy. So more happened in a half a day in my school than happened in that whole movie. So God has always been with me, okay, but it wasn't—but listen, He wants you—He wants you to pay attention to Him, and if you don't, He's gonna cause you to do it one way or the other if He loves you. If He doesn't love ya, s— He didn't like Cain, okay, Cain didn't make out good."

It's was amazing to me that he referred to the story in Genesis that had had such an effect upon me. He is referring more to Cain's murder itself than his punishment in living in the Land of Nod, but we had both been drawn to the same story. And it doesn't seem too much of a stretch to say that Cain was "broken" by God when he was exiled to Nod, east of Eden.

I was still interested in hearing more about how God had broken him in order to save him. He continued, "I'm gonna tell you something. That happened to me in Rikers Island years ago, when I took my little girl. She was being, uh, abused in a foster home. But that actually happened to me, but that—that's a very heavy experience. But in the hospital, in Corcoran, yes, I had a—I had a sec—in other words, God—in a sense, God spoke to me and He let me know, 'Listen, you're headed for a hard, hard time. Okay? Now, you got a choice now. You can either die in this prison, okay, or you keep having faith in Me and I'll bring you through it.'

"And I said, 'hard time.' A couple days after I had the encounter with the, uh, CO, okay, who never—who never came back to my room again, uh, what happened is, uh, I was released. I had died that night, and I, uh, the nurse told me she brought me back. A few days later I was released to an ambulance. They brought me to UCSD. And with—with the great care I got in UCSD, in one year—I was there for a year—semicoma. Okay? I was there for a year. Uh, I had a doctor tell me that, uh, he'd give me the operation, but I was gonna die anyway.

"And I told him, 'Listen, I've been in hell that'd burn the shoes off your feet in the first five minutes. I spent years there. There's nobody gonna kill me before God. God knows when I'll die, not you, brother.'

"He wouldn't operate on me. I'm not gonna give you his name. Let him go on in his career. But anyway, yes, I—and God—God— came to me and spoke to me. Okay? And believe me, He gave me an awakening. And He just told me, 'Listen, you got to change your ways. This is a part of history. We don't have much time left. Okay? Things are gonna happen. There's a storm coming. If you don't prepare—if you don't—if you don't maintain the greatest sanctuary, okay, against tyranny in the world, and keep tyrants from controlling it, then we're gonna lose it.'"

At the end of his story, he was referring to America. But he and I agree philosophically. When you say you're broken, you say to God, "Save me, and I'll do better. I'll walk the path you've laid out for me in the Bible. I'll turn my back on my previous, sinful life." An individual can save himself that way. So can a nation. And once it does, it can bring itself out of the hell it has created on Earth and into a more just, equitable, and godly life.

That certainly happened for Michael Hardy. His decision to change his life and his willingness to follow through were what saved him. As he went on to tell me, "I've changed my line of thinking. Okay? I, you know, I—I'm handicapped. I would travel around the streets in San Diego in my wheelchair. People treated me good—real, real good—real good. And, uh, and I—you know, I look at these people, these are the people, these are American people. These are good people. Okay? Who would want to hurt these people?

"You know, I'm not in the battle zone anymore. When you get out of the army, you stop fighting. Okay? I'm not in that army no more. I've been shot eleven times in the streets in this country. Okay? I've had sixteen gunfights, I've been in two major mafia gang wars, and that's only on this side of the border. Okay? But I'm gonna tell you something. When you don't need to do that, when you're not a combatant, then you look at the—you—you smell the flowers. And I—I thank God that I'm not here—you know, listen, I faced the gas chamber on my last case, and I beat three strikes three times by the grace of God only. And I—and you know what, you don't have to be a fool to sit around and compliment yourself and say, hey . . ."

I asked him what he would say if there were young kids listening to the show who might be gangbangers but who listen because they're different from their friends. Those kids would never admit they listen to Michael Savage, but I thought they might be listening because there was something there for them. For kids like that, tough as nails, in the street, doing what he had done as a kid, I asked Michael Hardy what he would say to them. Would he tell them it's the hero who puts the gun down?

Hardy replied, "Well, I would say—I would say that. I would definitely say that, but I'd say this also: when you see prison movies, you see two hours, *American Me*, or whatever else the prison movie is. Okay? If you want to go there, it's not gonna be two hours. It's gonna be millions and millions of seconds and minutes. Okay, millions of misery-packed time, okay, in a concentration camp setting where people concentrate on making your life

―――❈―――

$\mathfrak{T}$rain up a child in the way he should go,

And even when he is old, he will not depart from it.

—Proverbs 22:6

―――❈―――

miserable. Okay? They concentrate on doing that, whether it be the guards or the other inmates. You walk out, you don't know if there's gonna be a shooting. I was there when they fired eighteen shots in Corcoran on the yard. Okay? I watched people get stabbed in the mess hall. They start shooting the M14s, bullets are ricocheting. This is a hell that I can't understand anybody—and—and you're not fighting for anything. There's nothing worthy.

"It's not like what Audie Murphy did. Killed like, what, a hundred sixty Germans in twenty minutes? He did something here. Okay? It's not that. You're fighting for nothing. For people—your homeboys? You ain't gonna get a card from them. You ain't gonna get a letter from them. You ain't gonna get a grunion from them. Nothing. You're there alone.

"Make the decision. Make the decision before you cut that line and wind up in the Colorado River on the greatest rapids that you can ever imagine, and you're probably gonna drown in the mix. Make that decision. Stay home. Be true to your family. I've met a lot of—I met a lot of good kids in that—in this system I just came out. Good kids that are gonna spend the rest of their life, because of three strikes, in prison. And they got a lot of good values, they just need a little turn. And I'm gonna tell you something, they ain't gonna get it, because the biggest—the biggest maggots of the system here are the California Department of Corrections. They want three strikes because they want job security. So these kids that could do something, could be something, they need a break.

"You need to change the—some kind of learning system, whatever it is, okay, but you need to reach people. Waste all this energy and spend all this money on prisons and not school and not religious training, and take God out of the equation of this country. This is one country under God. When you take Him away, He's not above us anymore, you understand?"

And He shall judge between the nations,

And shall decide for many peoples;

And they shall beat their swords into plowshares,

And their spears into pruninghooks;

Nation shall not lift up sword against nation,

Neither shall they learn war any more.

— Isaiah 2:4

Yes, I understood exactly what he was saying. We lose our protection. And though Michael Hardy was ultimately 100 percent responsible for the crimes he committed, we can certainly do things to help future kids make better decisions than he did. It all starts with God. As individuals, as a nation, we must decide to seek Him out, to turn our backs on the sins of our past, and to follow through on doing His will. It's up to each one of us.

───⟨∞⟩───

And Job spoke, and said:

Let the day perish wherein I was born,

And the night wherein it was said:
'A man-child is brought forth.'

Let that day be darkness;

— Job: 3:2–4

───⟨∞⟩───

Loss

A lot of people are in pain right now. Everyone has lost something, either dear to them or that they believed in. People react differently to loss. For example, we see the madness of the progressives expressing their election loss with violence and hatred. What is loss but losing that which you once possessed or thought you possessed?

Consider what loss is. What has been the greatest loss in your life? How did you cope with it, be it of a loved one, a business, your pride, your dignity, your job, your promotion, your health? It's an interesting question to me because loss is part of life. Everyone thinks they're only going to win. They think that every time they throw the dice they're going to win. They're not.

I want to talk about this issue of loss, because a long time ago, back in the 1960s, when I was studying for my BS in science, there was a popular writer named Kahlil Gibran. He was a Lebanese Catholic writer who later converted to Baha'i, who lived between 1883 and 1931. He wrote a simple book called *The Prophet*. In it, he wrote on love, children, death, joy, and sorrow. My friends and I read and discussed him avidly. It shows you how different the generations are. So many of the young today

188 GOD, FAITH, AND REASON

are numb. They're frightened of life. They're frightened of love, not even knowing what love is or what loss is. Many of them are afraid to get a driver's license or take their place in society. They can't become adults.

A lot of people in America are hurting right now. Years ago, I wrote a book, and in it I told a story called "The Yarn Man Gets Cancer." It was about a man in the world in which I grew up, in Queens, New York. He was a poor man, as my father was. They were immigrants. They had probably come over on the same boat together. They had nothing; they were dirt poor. They lived fifteen to a room. I'm talking about cold-water flats on the Lower East Side before it became hip. It was a slum. Fifteen people lived in that man's apartment, his whole family that had come over from Europe together.

Well, they went out on the road of life here in America, that Yarn Man and my father. My father went down his road; the Yarn Man went down that road. They remained friends for life. The Yarn Man became wealthier than my father. He struck it big in a certain business that became fashionable, and he enjoyed his wealth. He bought a brand-new house out on Long Island, while we stayed in our little attached house in Queens.

My father did okay, but he never did great. That's okay. He always made a living, and my mother never had to work. She was a housekeeper and, believe me, a great one. It meant a big deal to us children. We didn't know how great it was to have a mother who was always there, who made sure that the sheets were clean, the meals were served, we did our homework, and did all the other things mothers do.

So the Yarn Man went on in life and made a lot of money. He opened a chain of wholesale stores. But then something happened. The trend that had made him wealthy changed. People no longer bought his product. He went bankrupt. He lost the house and had to move with his in-laws back to the tiny apartment he had lived in when he was an immigrant boy. He fell from Heaven to Earth.

I'd known him since I was a little kid. I'd always loved him. I loved all my father's friends and all my uncles. I loved everybody. It was an extended family. It was very warm and very close. This doesn't exist in America anymore, unless you are in an ethnic community or a very religious community. The sense of togetherness, the close-knit sense, is gone. Let me tell you something, it's beautiful when you have it. He was part of that for me. He was like a second uncle, father, whatever. We didn't separate it.

Many are the ills of the righteous,

But the LORD delivereth him out of them all.

—Psalms 34:19

I left New York, went out on my road, and came back. I left as a young man and came back a few years later. And there was this man, who had been very big in my mind, who had been wealthy, reduced to sitting in a chair in the living room in which I had grown up on Utopia Parkway, with tears in his eyes. He had a cigar in his hand—he was always a cigar smoker—and he looked at me with tears in his eyes and almost reached out and held my hand. He said, "Michael, Michael, look what happened to me. Look what happened to me. Did you hear what happened to me?" I said, "No, no, what happened, Barry?" He said, "I lost everything. I have nothing." He said, "I wish God had given me cancer rather than what He did to me." I didn't know what to say. I was stunned.

Well, I went out back on my road, I went back to my plant collecting, my graduate studies. I heard he got cancer a few months later and died. What is this story about? It's about how he took that loss internally and it killed him. He just couldn't cope with the loss. Yes, he was a cigar smoker, but there are many cigar smokers who don't get cancer. Cancer's a very interesting disease, and I don't want to go into that right now. We've all thought about it our whole life. If we're somewhere in the level of consciousness, we all think about diseases from time to time. What do you think all this obsession with food, vitamins, healthy living is about? It's trying to keep away the undertaker, isn't it?

Of course, he increased his risk of cancer with the cigars, but that's not what did it. When he lost his business, his dignity, and his pride, he was hollowed out inside, and nothing replaced it. As you well know, nature abhors a vacuum. And in his vacuum, some cells grew. Because that vacuum was not filled, the cells multiplied and divided. That's how cancer grew in him.

Again I'm asking you an esoteric question, which I realize doesn't have much to do with the news of the day. It isn't what people are talking about on the radio or in the newspaper. I'm asking you to consider what is the greatest loss in your life, because there's not an adult who has not lost something important. How have you coped with the loss, be it of a loved one, a business, your pride, your dignity, your job, your promotion, your health? You must have lost something. Humans lose things. Lots of people are in pain right now, and people react differently to loss.

The Lebanese poet and artist Khalil Gibran wrote about loss. He was a very tragic figure who died young and is best known for his classic 1923 book *The Prophet*. But for some reason, his writings touched my friends and me. We didn't know why at the time, but everyone was reading him in those days.

I particularly remember Gibran's writings on children, on joy and sorrow, and on love and on death. They were simple.

I'll give you a short example of what he wrote:

Your joy is your sorrow unmasked.
And the selfsame well from which your laughter rises
was oftentimes filled with your tears.

That's one of the things he wrote on joy and sorrow. What a great insight. Some of it was such great poetry. It's so true that joy would have little meaning without sorrow. Only the possibility of sorrow or disappointment can elevate the human soul to the heights of joy. And only hoping or wishing for joy can give definition to sorrow, which is the absence of joy. Are we not all like a wine cup fired in a potter's oven, burned by sorrow many times in our lives, only to be filled with wine at others?

The one poem I remembered the most, and I was young when I read this stuff, was his poem on children. We talked about this one and never forgot it. I still remembered it as I was raising my own children. It stays with me to this day.

Here is another short example of what Gibran wrote:

Your children are not your children.
They are the sons and daughters of life's longing for
itself....

192 GOD, FAITH, AND REASON

You are the bows from which your children
   as living arrows are sent forth.

I like the imagery of children being the arrows, parents the bows. Both are necessary, but once the bow has released the arrow, it can no longer control where the arrow goes. Everything has been done up to that point to put the arrow on the right path, but now the bow can only watch. Who's ever touched anything like this in his life? Not since the Bible itself has anything this good been written about children. I've read a lot in my life. I've read an awful lot of books. As a scholar working toward my master's degrees and my PhD, believe me, I read a lot of books. Back then I read a lot of scientific articles. I've read thousands and thousands and thousands of pages of stuff on the Internet since then. No one else has ever written about children like that.

Lo, children are a heritage of the Lord;

The fruit of the womb is a reward.

As arrows in the hand of a mighty man,

So are the children of one's youth.

Happy is the man that hath his quiver full of them;

They shall not be put to shame,

When they speak with their enemies in the gate.

—Psalms 127:3-5

The Meaning of Hanukkah

So why do Jews light candles for eight nights? It used to be a joke that Christian kids get gifts on only one day during the holidays and Jews get gifts on eight nights. It used to be a joke between Christians and Jews. It was very cute. See, in those days, you could joke about religions and everyone still got along. Then a meanness came into this country like you cannot believe. An ill wind was brought in that makes people hate every other religion.

So what is Hanukkah? What's its meaning to you? Is it a kids' holiday? You light candles, get gifts, spin a dreidel.

The story goes that in ancient times the Jewish temple was sacked by the Romans. And when the Jews went back to the temple, they went through the rubble and looked for the holy oil that had been used to light the lamps. The oil was supposed to last only one night, but it lasted for eight.

What is the symbolism of such a story, even for those who are hopeless and have no religion whatsoever? It has tremendous symbolic power. It means that when you think all is lost, when you think you can't go on, when you think there's no hope, somewhere within you there is a holy oil that can still be lit. It can still light the fire within you. You must learn to always look for that holy oil within yourself. It's there in the rubble of your being. No matter how destitute you are, no matter how broken you are, no matter how horrible your life appears to be, even if you don't think you can take another second of it, stop for one minute and take a deep breath. Think of the deep resonance that put you here and put your ancestors here.

You weren't born unto yourself. You're the end line of millions of years of evolution. Countless thousands of generations of human beings produced you. What a waste it would be for you to go away, wouldn't it? To kill yourself with drugs or alcohol or some other way?

So you say to yourself, wait a minute, I can't just waste this incredible gift I was given, this gift of life. So you start to think, okay, all those generations that preceded me, dig into the rubble. Dig into the rubble of your being and look for that oil inside you, the holy oil, and reignite it.

That's the true meaning of Hanukkah. I think it's a beautiful story. It has no religious connotation in any way, but it has a tremendous power of giving anyone who's looking to find it something within themselves to go on. It's been written by poets in many other ways. Read Rudyard Kipling, and you'll know what I'm talking about, the man who fights for the last ounce of strength. Every fighter knows it, every runner knows it, everyone in the field of battle knows it: you can reach into yourself and find something more.

Witness to the First Moment

Not to trivialize a sacred day, not to remove the power of abstinence did I find myself first resisting the commandment to fast, and later, years later, after "coming back," I resisted my teacher's temptation to *enjoy* food on this holiest of holy days!

As a rebellious kid, I once sped past my Queens temple in a gray and narrow AC Bristol on an autumn gold Yom Kippur. Blasting the exhaust to shock the congregants into noticing me, I awoke to the realization, about twenty years later, that by turning my back on my congregation, I had created my own exile. Loneliness and alienation may be good fuel for the searcher. Once discovered, a worthwhile goal should reward the seeker with a place, *his* place in time—and hopefully, reentry into his "group" or congregation.

In my case, nothing of the kind happened. Forever addicted to the sense of isolation that had sustained me in my travels, I became unable or unwilling to join *any* group, except the occasional Passover celebrants I somehow managed to connect with from Fiji to Jerusalem.

Rabbi Zadok said:

Separate not thyself from the congregation; . . . make not
of the Torah a crown wherewith to aggrandize thyself nor
a spade wherewith to dig.

Then I found myself in a suicidal phase, a crisis congealed by
piling too many "life stresses" into one brief month of my life.

Then, at the moment of my daughter Rebecca's birth, *seeing*
life oozing from life, witnessing the first moment, I faced directly
the *fact* of the *last moment*, my mortality.

Unusual only in the Western world, this male distancing
from birth? Not so! Prohibitions abound. Men in many cultures
are forewarned to stay away. Yet millions have attended and do
attend this rite of passage without experiencing an emotional cat-
aclysm. But for Jewish men descended from *kohan*s (priests), this
moment, among others, is strictly taboo.

Do not contact a corpse, nor witness a fetus to life. Why?

Perhaps our ancient priests abstained from some of life's
most poignant moments to maintain their intellectual distance
and objectivity. However, perhaps this distancing, this aversion
to life's messier moments, established a too-intellectual Judaism
bearing a sea of dry teachings, devoid of meaning to an unbridled
meanderer.

And I wept with my soul with fasting,

And that became unto me a reproach.

—Psalms 69:11

With Cuban music cajoling Rebecca out and keeping my nerve steady, I was encouraged beyond the antechamber into the room of the womb's unfolding offering.

There were three women in white and my wife, Janet, the man an invited, hesitant stranger. No longer playing his music, his words sealed behind a mask, evolution's voluptuous force emerged.

Placenta brought to his eyes by the lady doctor, her nurse, our midwife looking at the stranger.

Repulsed and dizzy, this was no longer biology laboratory. I accepted my mortal fate and somewhat confusedly withdrew after thanking God for safe passage.

Soon after, I had my own rite of passage, a terminal degree in philosophy from a university too prestigious to be less than final.

In this way, the world of life and death is created by the mind, in bondage to the mind, we are ruled by the mind; the mind is the master of every situation. The world of suffering is brought about by the deluded mind.

Therefore, all things are primarily controlled and ruled by the mind, and are made up by the mind. As the wheels follow the ox that draws the cart, so suffering follows the mind that surrounds itself with impure thoughts and worldly passions.

—DHARMA; UMMAGGA-SUTTA, DHAMMAPADA

Dancing with Chasids

The narrow, worn wooden floorboards creaked as the widening circle of dancing men revolved, stepping nimbly, their arches stretched in contradiction to the clumsy, old-fashioned, dull black shoes.

"The whole year happy, the whole year happy, the whole year happy for me and you and me," went the loud refrain.

Dancing within that circle with my son, Russell, sitting atop my shoulders, I came face-to-face with a red-haired, green-eyed young teacher, dancing with his son rocking above, all of us touching the next man's shoulders. It was the end of the long prayer service for that Sabbath eve, traditionally marked with a circle of dancing and loud singing; the women, on *their* side of the curtain, joining in their own levity to welcome the "Sabbath Queen."

Eating and drinking were always a favorite release for me, and I began to gravitate to Chabad House in Berkeley on Friday nights after Rebecca's birth, telling my nonreligious friends that it was the best place I knew of to eat and drink with my family. Somehow isolated in impersonal restaurants, I *felt* better eating among Jewish people who seemed only too happy to accept us.

That acceptance, I realized years later, was always tentative and predicated on our "returning" to their Orthodox ways. True,

Thou shalt eat, but not be satisfied;

And thy sickness shall be in thine inward parts;

And thou shalt conceive, but shalt not bring forth;

— Micah 6:14

the rabbis and many of their disciples seemed to genuinely love the glint in my eyes, my humor, and my happiness in helping serve the communal festive meal. Our souls *were* interconnected, but as the years turned without my becoming a convert, still dancing and singing and eating and serving on the occasional Sabbath, a new mood was detected.

Disappointment? Rejection? Condemnation? I slowly lost interest in this too-rigid form of Judaism.

The turning point in my removal occurred when I accidentally took a bottle of vodka[4] to a Passover seder and was publicly admonished, first by the rabbi's son (a mere boy) and later, in the vestibule, by the red-haired rabbi himself.

Angered, I stormed into the packed dining hall and shouted, "He who insults a fellow man in public, it is as though he has killed him!" (a precept from the Talmud), followed, for emphasis, "I will not be crucified by a traffic cop dressed as a teacher!"

Shocked by my apparent rudeness, the congregants stared in disbelief as I brusquely took the children's hands and bristled out of there.

Their orthodoxy, Barry later told me, was what had driven *him* from his orthodox upbringing into the Hillel or "liberal" wing of the Jewish bird. When he had first chosen that path, as a late teenager, the Orthodox tribe's members had picketed his father's house, declaring a death in the family!

"That's why I had my cook prepare some food for us today," he said with a smile on that Yom Kippur day. "So we can *enjoy* God, instead of fearing."

---

[4] Vodka was always an acceptable and welcome drink at dinners and certain rabbinical study sessions among this largely Russian Jewish group. I was unaware that a special vodka (kosher for Passover) was required.

At first, I only watched him eating that delicious eggplant cas-serole. It had taken me so many years to "come back," even in part, that I was reluctant to turn away again. This was months *after* the Passover fiasco, and I was observing with Barry alone, no longer drawn by Chabad.

If a diver is to secure pearls he must descend to the bot-tom of the sea, braving all dangers of jagged coral and vicious sharks. So, man must face the perils of worldly passion if he is to secure the precious pearl of Enlighten-ment. He must first be lost among the mountainous crags of egoism and selfishness, before there will awaken in him the desire to find a path that will lead him to Enlighten-ment. —DHARMA

There are seven marks of an uncultured, and seven of a wise man. The wise man does not speak before him who is greater than he in wisdom; and does not break in upon the speech of his fellow; he is not hasty to answer; he questions according to the subject matter, and answers to the point; he speaks upon the first thing first, and the last last; regarding that which he has not understood he says, I do not understand it; and he acknowledges the truth. The reverse of all this is to be found in an uncultured man. —ANONYMOUS

Jerome's Story

I want to reiterate, I'm not a particularly religious man. I was raised in an atheistic household. My father was an atheist from Russia and my mother was a kind of very faithful believer—not religious, but she knew God existed. She did things that made me understand that. Tragedy befell the whole family. But the way she dealt with it was one thing; the way my father dealt with it was another. The way I deal with it is yet another. I learned to be a speaker because of my mother's sadness and tragedy.

My mother was deeply saddened by what had happened to my brother. She couldn't fathom what had happened. She'd had a healthy daughter, then a healthy son—me—and then another boy who looked perfectly fine. He had blond hair, blue eyes; he looked perfectly normal. But after a short period of time, they found out he was not normal. He couldn't see, couldn't hear, and couldn't speak. He was basically a vegetable, or so they thought.

It wrecked the whole family. My mother cried endlessly. No one else knew that. And what does a little boy do when a mother is crying? He tries to make her happy.

So I would entertain her. I would do stupid things. I became an entertainer for my mother. I'd imitate people. I'd put on faces.

I'd make sounds and noises, and I'd wipe the tears away. She'd stop crying. She would smile.

If you read my book *Teddy and Me*, you may remember the story about my brother, Jerome. I loved him very much. I learned to talk and to entertain because of the tragedy with my brother.

So it affected me in that way. I learned to entertain my mother. And, as you can see, I can go from the maudlin to the enraged in one second. In one second I can turn from a kind of maudlin, sad guy into an enraged bull. It all rages inside my soul, and in that sense I'm very much alive, from top to bottom.

But I also learned how to talk to audiences and animals because of my silent brother. I wrote about this in one of my books. Everyone said, "Don't talk to him." He was sitting in a high chair, strapped in. They told me he was blind and deaf and couldn't speak. And when no one was looking, I would sneak into the kitchen to talk to him.

Let me tell you how primitive medicine was in the 1940s. They told me, the healthy brother, "Don't talk to your brother. You'll bother him." I thought, if he's deaf, how can I bother him? He can't hear me. So I would talk to him anyway because I loved him. I just loved him so much. And I would whistle to him because I didn't think he could understand words. And he would smile when I whistled to him. So I said, wait a minute, if he can understand the whistle, he knows his brother's here.

Then I'd hear the voice: "Michael? Michael, what are you doing in there? Are you bothering Jerome? Come on, get out of there."

Later, the backward doctors of the day decided that for the sake of the healthy children, he would have to go to a home. I want you to think about the profound impact on the "healthy children," who felt responsible for sending him to hell.

Then the eyes of the blind shall be opened,

And the ears of the deaf shall be unstopped.

Then shall the lame man leap as a hart,

And the tongue of the dumb shall sing;

— Isaiah 35:5–6

The day came when they had to take him to a state home. It was a horrible place on Staten Island. I can't remember the name of the home. It was a snake pit that was exposed as horrible years later. Do you think the VA hospitals are bad? They took away this little, helpless, five-year-old boy because the doctors were such quacks in those days.

In those days, where we lived, everyone knew everyone else. I lived in a tenement in the Bronx. I can't remember if it was six or eight stories. But everybody knew everybody. It was like a Satyajit Ray movie. If you've ever watched Indian movies about India, Calcutta, the teeming masses, well, that's my childhood. Those were the days when you'd see women sitting outside in front of the building in chairs, just like in those old black-and-white movies, watching as the children played in the streets.

In the summer, they'd open the hydrants so the kids could run through the water. That was our swimming pool, the gutter and the water. It felt good to me. I enjoyed it. It was cold—and fresh. And the women would protect you from any potential danger. But there was no potential danger there because nobody sped down the street. There were no guns going off, and perverts were thrown off the top of a building. If there was even a hint of a perv in a neighborhood, the men would find him and they would throw him off a building. So there were no pervs around. The men in my neighborhood didn't wait for a judge to tell them what they could do. They'd either beat a perv up or threw him off a building. So we had a very safe childhood in that sense.

So everyone knew everyone else. And the day comes. Everyone hears that they're taking away my brother. Everybody is in the street. There's crying. And there's sadness. The whole neighborhood sees this going on. My uncle, a strong man, breaks down and cries like an infant right there in front of everyone. And my little brother is taken away in an ambulance. I don't even know who took him. Two men in white. That was the beginning of something, and it was also the end of something.

What am I supposed to believe? That God made a mistake? It was just a mistake in the hospital? Somebody made a mistake somewhere and they did this to him? Or it was a neurological defect that created my brother and there was no reason for him?

I believe he was created like that for me. I believe my brother was created that way for me to be as articulate and as impassioned as I am. In that sense, I feel very guilty. I must live for two people. I've told you that before. Otherwise, there's no explanation for me to be alive this long, not with my genetic inheritance and not with the stress level I've lived with. I should've been dead a long time ago. But the point is that God had a certain fate for me and I think it had to happen, that my brother had to be punished for me to live the way I am. Would you believe that?

And Joseph fell upon his father's face,
and wept upon him, and kissed him.

And Joseph commanded his servants the
physicians to embalm his father. And the
physicians embalmed Israel.

And forty days were fulfilled for him; for so are
fulfilled the days of embalming. And the Egyptians
wept for him threescore and ten days.

— Genesis 50:1–3

My Father's Death

It's been almost fifty years since my father was found dead in his store. I didn't know all the circumstances, nor did I care to inquire. At the time, I was living in Honolulu, six thousand miles away, pursuing my own dreams.

Not long ago I got off the telephone with my cousin Sam, who told me for the first time that it was he who had closed my father's eyes, removed his wedding and other rings, taken the cash out of the safe and bundled it up for my mother, and so on. I didn't know all the details.

Strange how it came up in the conversation. It was a quiet Saturday afternoon here in California, and I was just thinking about the few relatives I have left on the earth and how my cousin Sam had always been my favorite. I had forgotten that although he had graduated college and was quite brilliant, perhaps smarter than I, he had gone into his father's store in the antiques market where my father also had a store.

In any case, one word led to another and he said, "Don't you remember? It was I who found your father." I said, "No, tell me the circumstances," which he did.

I said, "How did you know he was dead?"

He said, "He had a little Italian guy working for him in the stand named Tony. It was a busy Sunday, the kind of Sunday you wanted. People were teeming in and out of the market. The streets were full. Everyone was buying. Tony came out; his face looked white and he said, 'Your uncle. Your uncle.'"

Sam continued, "I went in there, and your father was slumped on the floor."

I said, "What do you mean, slumped? He was lying down?"

He said, "No, he was sitting down in the back of the store, the little stall in the store, with his back to the wall and his head to the side. I went in, and his face was blue and his lips were blue and his head was to the side. I dashed out to my father in the midst of the busy store, and I said, 'Dad, Uncle Benny is dead.' He said, 'What do you mean? What, are you crazy?' 'No,' I said. 'His face is blue.'"

Sam said, "My father didn't even want to go in and look. He said, 'You better go in there and take all the valuables before the cops get there. They'll clean him out.' Sam did just that. "I went in and took your father's rings off, his watch, his wallet. The safe was open. I bundled up whatever cash was in there. It wasn't a lot—a few thousand dollars, maybe. Put it in an envelope for your mother. Took it out. We called the police. That's the whole story in a nutshell."

I told Sam, "Well, live and learn. I had no idea." I asked him, "Who notified my mother? Who was at home in Queens in the little attached house?"

Sam replied, "I don't really know, but by the time we got home, your house was full of people. Everybody was there, like your uncle, your aunt, and neighbors. Full. Your mother was on the couch lying down."

I thought to myself, God, what a different world it was. Everyone was there. In my world, living alone as I do, no one will even know when I die. I have millions of listeners, and I'll die alone. And here he was, a humble immigrant, surrounded by family and friends. Who was the richer man? The immigrant or the immigrant's son? I'll let you, my dear readers, decide.

$\mathfrak{T}$hou shalt not take vengeance, nor bear any grudge

against the children of thy people, but thou shalt love

thy neighbour as thyself: I am the LORD.

— Leviticus 19:18

Rabbi in a Brothel
(a Fable)

"**E**ither become a rabbi or open a brothel in Borneo," I told my wife. "That's what my choices are." I had reached the ultimate cul-de-sac in my misbegotten existence. "Staying on this road is decay, disease, and death, straight ahead. I'd rather become a rabbi or open a brothel."

"I agree with you totally," she replied. "Both would be closer to God than this."

"What would you do if I *did* decide to take off to Borneo or a seminary?"

"I'd move into the rental house, work part-time, and go to grad school somewhere in the area."

"Well, as the old beatniks used to say, 'At least my manuscripts and other stuff would all be in one place.'"

Our situation was well beyond retrofit beatnik. We owned *two* modest houses in Marin County, California, but were renting and living in a third, in a better neighborhood on the water, with a dock. The dock had stood empty for almost a year. We had sold the boat after an accident. A Chinese fortune-teller had predicted it, but we had taken his prescience as you would a fortune cookie.

Basing his predictions on complex ancient Chinese books with geometric charts, Lin Yutang would write out your coming year on a monthly basis, in brief capsules, such as:

Feb.: "Friend or partner with company, house energy weak."

April: "Working very hard, watch out and avoid conflict with wife."

The previous year, he had warned me:

Dec.: "Money out for parent's health."

East to the seminary in Cleveland or west to a Borneo of dark images in Conradian relief? A rickety bamboo structure on a river. Bar girls. Fans. Flickering reminiscences of Cobra gunships. Of Charlie. If not love, maybe satisfaction born of an atypical end for a boy from the Bronx.

I packed my mental sea bag and drove over the Gate, still sighing at the sight of the sharp cliffs, the bay churning as it fought the incoming sea, the Farallons beyond. I was heading for the union hall to ship out, in my case the booking agent for the Royal Viking Line. I had an open invitation to travel first class on any of their ships, in any port I asked, at any time. My pay? Lectures. Lectures and my rare color slides of the South Pacific Islands taken on my travels since 1968. I'd sailed on each of the company's beautiful liners many times. I had won the hearts of the old cardiac and cancer crowd while managing to please the Norwegian captains and Swedish and Finnish stewardesses with my insights not into investments but into medicinal botanicals in the islands.

෴

> **H**e that breatheth forth truth uttereth righteousness;
>
> But a false witness deceit.
>
> —Proverbs 12:17

෴

I'd climbed Rain Mountain on Western Samoa and been photographed lying adjacent to Robert Louis Stevenson's tomb, only my head jutting from the cement. I'd kissed Paul Gauguin's grave in the Marquesas, drinking a $300 bottle of red Bordeaux alone that night, listening to the long breaking surf rolling onto the reef- less island, all the way from the nearest continent five thousand miles distant. I'd had my testicles held in an assessing way by wild mountain warriors in New Guinea who still behaved according to the original meaning of "testament." (As you spoke, they held your balls feeling the resonance or lack thereof to judge your honesty.)

And in the Cook Islands, a break in the outlying reef in the middle of a storm meant just clearing the razorlike coral on a small wooden boat, getting stuck there after our fifty-four-foot cutter had been sunk by an accidental blow from a passing sub. I remember sitting for weeks on that little atoll, pondering William Marsten's grave. Marsten was an English mariner who settled on Palmerston Island, had four wives, and fathered twenty-three children, whose descendants now took care of me. Sweet inbreds, these, violating the predictions of geneticists and royal watchers.

Yeah. I'd seen some adventure without thieving or killing. I'm an anomaly of the last years of the millennium, I know, but real.

I'd left New York for Honolulu in 1968 and now missed my relatives, living and dead, who were more real to me than a serrated black-and-white photo but unreachable in their time and conditions. Each, ossified by life, thought of me, if ever, as a friendly black sheep who had jumped the family fence, never to return.

Always good for a chuckle was old Bob, who was always available, anytime day or night, for a mooch, a free beer or plate of food, but mainly to shoot the breeze. It was usually me talking rapid-fire New Yorkese and he responding in his slow East Bay, self-taught way.

"'Well, a man who'd go to sea for fun'd go to hell for a pastime,' said the quartermaster, drinking his gin," said Bob (quoting Lowry) after I told him of my plan to ship out as lecturer to some ports, any ports, for a few weeks.

"Bob," I said. "Bob, I can't take it anymore. I have impulses I'm afraid of, to hurt myself and others, my mind's abuzz with scores of vengeful thoughts, towards everyone I know and ever knew."

Again, he threw a quote at me: "Who knows what delicate wonders have disappeared from the world for want of the will to survive."

"Cut the crap, Bob! You've been reading too many cheap novels in that room of yours."

❧

A man's pride shall bring him low;

But he that is of a lowly spirit shall attain to honour.

—Proverbs 29:23

"No, not a novel. From *Enter the Dragon* with Bruce Lee," Bob replied.

"Are you kidding?" I said. "I thought you never watched TV in your life."

"I heard it from Peter, the cook over at Tong Kiang," Bob answered.

"A great mind, that Peter," I replied, sarcasm straightening my twisted mouth.

I looked up to salute the human vision and courage it had taken to throw this span across the bay as I sped under the North Tower. The familiar dull orange girders were brushed by light fog, giving me a clear shot at the tower lights.

Images rolled through my mind, of past cruises to the southern hemisphere. I could see the blue Nordic eyes of the German captain as he paced the deck, his unshaven face in a grimace of doubt, looking mad. He surprised me in only an undershirt and unshaven that dawn as I awoke in a particularly hard roll, my far-forward cabin taking a pounding that sounded like sledgehammers against the steel plate that separated me and my sleeping family from the Tonga Trench, six thousand miles down.

The captain stared at me on the deck, with half-mad eyes, bellowing and pleading, "Lecturer, all the time, Tahiti to Fiji, Fiji to Tahiti, Tahiti to Fiji, Fiji to Tahiti," his Saxon English a perfect cadence for the boredom of this cruise. A fixed back-and-forth cruise for a man longing to be free to sail the high seas, for the asylum bound, I'm sure. But poor Captain Aye (I swear it!) didn't quite take that desperate route.

After that storm subsided, he must have accepted his tame lot because I saw him that night, at dinner, all cleaned up and immaculate, personifying the German sea captain.

Hitting the brakes, I almost swerved into the guardrail to avoid careening across the roadway! Another Bay airhead cutting me off from the *right-hand* lane and now pretending she didn't do a thing by staring dead straight ahead. I'll speed up now, there. Good, "F—— you, you rotten jerk! You like to cut people off? Here, how'd you like to swim to San Francisco!"

Okay. Calming down in the slow-moving traffic now, my thoughts returned to the sea. Once, when our ship docked in Recife, I took a small group of the more adventurous passengers into the jungle to show them medicinal plants firsthand. "This one cures headaches, that one ulcers. Memory is enhanced with this," and so on.

One particularly grating skeptic kept lecturing me. "Even if these plants *do* work, how do you know it's not all psychological?" With a putz like him, no amount of scientific references would be convincing.

"Here, let me show you something." I began to climb a huge hardwood tree while continuing to talk to the shrinking group below. "You see this vine," I shouted. "If you take the sap and put it in an arrow and shoot a monkey high on a tree (gasps of liberal horror), the monkey will fall from the tree into the hands of the hungry hunter below." I continued to climb to find a particularly beautiful flowering sample of the curare vine.

"So," shouted the putz, "what's the point?"

"This vine contains the drug curare. It's a muscle relaxant. It makes *any* animal lose its grip. Monkey, man, New Yorker, Hoosier, priest, dancer, cardiac patient . . . get it?" I bellowed. "No matter who you are, the curare will have the same effect on your muscles. It's not at all in your head. It's biological, physiological. Wait, I'll be down in a minute to show you."

Pulling myself up a few more feet, I was through the dense canopy of the tree. In a blink, as in a fantasy, I was on solid ground!

A pack of dogs came running at me. I froze. There was a glacial-like pool of clear blue water, and from beyond it a female shouted, "Don't worry, they're harmless."

The bridge cables whipped past, his eyes now in their ever-ascending arc. Halfway across, he wondered, just what impelled him on?

In those reveries just past, he realized that in those previous trips to the islands he had very much been running *toward*, toward goals. Now he would be, in fact was, running *from*. From all that California or at least the Bay Area had become. From all that the *world* according to the synods had become. ABC + CBS + NBC + CNN = HATEFUL! From all that the rotting sick deviates had made in their own image. A city built on Judeo-Christian values, on Italian and Irish Catholic virtues, on Jewish business acumen, Chinese labor and investments—all this beauty had been stalled by a whore. Where once there was genuine pride, the pride of genuine accomplishments, there now was hawked in its place all the false pride of the progressives and then some.

The false pride of being a pervert.

∽✤∾

And, behold, the LORD passed by, and a great and strong wind rent the mountains, and broke in pieces the rocks before the LORD; but the LORD was not in the wind;

—First Kings 19:11

∽✤∾

The false pride of "civil rights" lawsuits.

The false pride of first birthing and then laying the blame for some epidemics on innocent bystanders.

The false pride of superior culture.

The false pride of calumny—in the arts—literature—academia (wherever the perverts reigned).

The false pride of sexual freedom marked by the clanking of chains.

Yes, it had become a time of falseness. A time to cry, a time to weep, a time to leap, a time to run.

"Time is the great sorter of experience." That's what Lin Yutang, his fortune teller, had last sent him.

From nowhere came that anagram. Would time give him the perspective needed to sort these emotions? To separate his *own* condition in time from that of the city in which he lived? Had the forces of present-tense communication made him a direct emblem of his city, of his country, of his time? Without a moment anymore to dwell on the past, neither his own nor the historical realities of anything, it seemed—just the newspapers, thirty-six television channels, mindless news updates on the car radio— he had become a point in time. The recipient of bad forebodings. Of riots and crashes and fires and streams of racial beatings not seen nor heard since Hitler's Germany. Oh, how this poor, running rabbi needed the sanctity of an honest brothel! He *had* to run or else risk falling into madness. The madness of a John Wilkes Booth, whose self-realized cowardice became blamed on just one man, the one who had taken credit for "freeing the slaves" whom Booth had marked for death.

Should he stay, he might focus on the loudest of them now strutting about city chambers. And only God knew where that might lead.

"He was hurt by God, so he will become a priest" was a saying he'd grew up on. His younger brother, born a cripple, was supposed to become a holy man but had died at age seven. So he, his older brother, had somehow felt obligated to fulfill his poor brother's calling. But how?

With the impulses of a not-so-ordinary man and the personality of a born tyrant, our bridge traveler to nowhere had no intention of spending his life dressed in black.

But could he not climb a tree so high and see so far as to bring back to Earth for all to see God's vision for a perfect South? Could he not somehow fulfill his brother's lost lot in other than a formal priestly way? By rescuing healing plants, for example? Oh, how impossible this quest of the alternate priest became, to prove to God, if not to man, that you worshipped Him, but in your own way! To do so without edifice or pageant. To sing his praises in silence. To bow down to Him without moving. To follow his commandments without following them. (Had our running priest become a Buddhist?)

"The Messiah is here!" proclaimed the flyers. And now it seemed his religious Jewish friends of the Lubavitcher sect had all gone mad! Souls that had once, years before, sheltered him, saved him from madness, from suicide or homicide. But now they too, it seemed, needed saving! "Collective insanity," he had thought when first he saw their announcements. To not only cry out for the Coming (in Jewish eyes) but to publish a date and then, when the day had passed, drop all reference to the Chosen One!

Gender, God, and reality. Heavy stuff to balance on a bridge.

A horn warned the fog. A ship slipped the gate. Images of Bob and his generation looking forward to the shore crossed his mind. "I'm on a bus going to Fort Cronkite. It comes to the end of the line. The driver says, 'Everybody off the bus.' I sit still. 'Okay, off the bus.'"

"I ain't getting off," I tell him. "It's too windy on the beach." (Too windy even for an old salt.) For June in San Francisco, we're having August weather, but worse. The product of Saddam's oil fires last year? Vectors of wind out of control. The Moslem winds again? For in just a hundred years, remember, our cunning Arab cousins took an unknown local cult of the Book and swept two-thirds of the world.

He gets out of his driver's seat. He comes to the back of the bus where I'm sitting next to two old ladies. "Look," he says, "you've got to get off the bus."

"I ain't going."

He's got a half-shaved head, an earring, three rings on each finger, and he's a bus driver!

One word leads to another. "Listen, I'm gonna smoke and you've got to get off the bus!"

"Well," I told him, "it's illegal. Get off the bus and smoke with the rest of the numbskulls. I'm not getting off in this wind."

Wind. *Hasim.* Screws everybody's mind. Ions? Blows pollen, mites, viroids into people's minds? Sweeps protective cullens from the skin? *Upraises particles unseen stripping people?*

Wind. Wind is death. According to the Japanese.

Wind. The Russians think it brings illness. As do the Chinese. Not a race on Earth welcomes it, yet wind is the great pollinator without which all screws itself.

Wind. The world itself upsets.

So Bob stays on the bus with the two old ladies, one asking the other, "What did he say?" not comprehending the bus driver or seeing his earrings or shaved head or attitude. The hostile driver smokes a cigarette.

But the fog was wafting strong now, in the middle of the bridge.

Bob sat firm in his triumph over one little vandal. It was his most recent battle against evil, one that had begun on the mean streets of East Oakland and led through Guadalcanal. I fought my own battles against evil, becoming myself, one who, as I often jested, had had to learn to "lie, cheat, and steal" (or was it "beg, borrow, and steal"?) to survive. Despite all my advanced degrees, my many published and unpublished books, and my obvious verbal talents, society hid its rewards from me. The vandals had broken through the gates of academia, journalism, publishing, medicine, law, and government. And in their thirty-year reign, they had created an "old vandals" network not seen in America since the bureaucratic tyrannies of the early part of this century, more like the current social order in Sicily, where neither talent nor education counted, or the recent experience in eastern Europe.

Could the warnings and exhortations of Job compare with Disney? Could Jeremiah compete with the evening news?

Look what the *Times* had become. One power-mad psychopath after another paraded throughout, with all the details of his/her personal wealth displayed so as to render the moderately successful reader impotent and hopeless by the time the sports page was reached. Could this epic of the Sulzbergers be compared with Ecclesiastes?

No, of course not.

Which is why the original book of the Jews was now read only by illiterate fools, who by circumstance or genetic dysfunction believed the words had been dictated from Heaven and inscribed in stone. Probably a collection of constipated poets, failed jewel hustlers, bankrupt sandal makers, whoremongers past their prime, child molesters, animal torturers, and other biblical-age riffraff, thought the bridge driver as he now approached the South Tower, nearing the toll booths into the city.

He glanced at the tiny fortune-cookie fortune Scotch-taped to the dashboard of his old two-door Bronco: "You are an angel—beware of those who collect feathers."

By now it's a private comedy. I'm no angel, but I've lost most of my feathers, mostly *trying* to fly, he mused. Every time I've been given a chance I could soar like an eagle—it's been the *trying* to fly where the real losers live. Those failed writers who became agents now all menopausal and ready to give to the UJA after years supporting the PLO. Those tight-lipped WASP academics whose guilt made them hire the Jews after the Holocaust, the academic Jews who chose to exile any hint of rebellion in their Jewish *male* descendants, welcoming instead the women and other minorities they thought they could bamboozle. And bamboozle they did, running every racket known to the mafia within the halls of academe, encouraging all the while the debate over "affirmative action" so they could continue their plunder—plundering unnecessary research funds, conducting excessive animal experimentation, molesting their young students, holding grandiose conferences modeled on the tools of those governmental bureaucrats they did business with, the "Look what the universities have become," he thought; plunderer of graduate students' discoveries and labor, plunderer of all lost ideals everywhere and in all time since Abraham tried to slay Isaac but was saved by a counterhallucination. A generation of incompetents not seen in the history of the republic, incompetents who had created their own fields of study to justify their lack of productive scholarship in the real fields of learning. Those fertile fields which blossomed with a flora so vibrant and diverse, now reduced in size and offering to "women's studies," "black studies," "Chicano studies," "lesbian studies," "gay studies," "trans studies," all nonsciences created by jingoists with tenure desperate for attention and respect.

Leo Tolstoy wrote somewhere that those who believe their religion is greater than God will believe that their sect is greater than their religion and end up by believing that they are greater than their sect.

On and on it went as he drove over the Golden Gate Bridge.

For if a man live many years,

Let him rejoice in them all,

And remember the days of darkness,

For they shall be many.

All that cometh is vanity.

— Ecclesiastes 11:8

The Room with a
View to Eternity

Yearning for the occasional conversation and the soft
sweet winter light as it bathes the pastel-colored wooden
buildings, the wonderful food of China and Italy as it
has been adapted to America's West Coast over a period of about
a hundred years—that is a century of mixing local vegetables and
soils into the ancient recipes of the Hakka people, the Genovese,
and at least one Sicilian—I rented a room in North Beach.

Walking up the stairs to my room on the top floor of the old
five-story hotel on Sansome Street at Broadway, I ran into my old
friend. "Hey, if it isn't my old friend Bob," I said, greeting him at
the top of the first set of stairs of the redbrick walk-up. The lino-
leum was as clean as your grandmother's, and it always reminded
me of my grandmother's big house with the potted palm by the
door. A grandmother dead now for more than forty years, whose
house emitted a clean, sweet aroma that I swear I recognize each
time I enter this random hotel occupied mainly by men on the run
or hiding from their past.

Bob and I hadn't spoken on the phone for about three
months, since I had moved into my house. He had used to call a

couple times a week, but being a notoriously cheap bastard, he had stopped calling because the rate was no longer local.

"So, Bob, I'm now forty-seven cents away. Too much, heh?"

He gave me his John Wayne smile, which suited his face and lanky sixty-five-year-old frame.

I think we had stopped speaking a few months earlier after I had given him a few free bottles of reishi mushroom and he hadn't even offered to buy me a beer. For Christ's sake, when people couldn't pay the county doctor in the American town of the distant past, they had given him a barrel of apples.

But I had saved him from sure death at the claws of cancer more than ten years before, and the bond was too sure to break over a temporary impasse. By taking him from the VA hospital up on the bluff overlooking the Golden Gate and putting him on thirty grams of vitamin C a day plus other vitamins and a diet and some herbs, I'd pulled him back from the diagnosis of lymphoma and going home to die, the best the doctors could offer.

"Bob, I went to a funeral last week for my friend Joel's father. You want to hear about it? I almost called you to come. They didn't have too many friends."

He nodded, sipped on his beer, and settled back to listen. One thing about his generation and his culture, they were good listeners.

"Joel's father, Murray, was eighty-two," I began. "He survived Auschwitz, where the German bastards cut three fingers from his right hand with a saw, just for sport."

I watched Bob's face. It was as I expected, guarded. After all, I had met him in a bar about twelve years before, when I had stood up to his anti-Semitic ravings. We quickly became good but guarded pals, he needing his Jew and I my goy. Though he stood over six feet five inches and was made of lean English muscle, I had threatened to kill him if he didn't shut up.

Now, I'm only five feet seven, but I'm broad enough and my eyes relay protons of dark danger. I've been mistaken for an Italian in Italy, a Spaniard in Spain, an Arab in Morocco, a Jew in Brooklyn. The reason I say I've been "mistaken" for a Jew is because I don't behave like one, at least those I know here in America. Maybe I was born to lead a tank brigade in Israel or a mob in Vegas. All I know is that I've led Little League in the suburbs and a few expeditions to collect plants in the Fiji Islands and been damn proud of it. But my eyes are those of a saint when calm, a killer when agitated. It's in my blood, I think, this murderous rage. Either through eye power or the work of saving angels, I've talked my way out of death more than once.

So Bob shut his mouth that night many years ago, and, as I've said, he tends to harbor certain Nazi sentiments. So when I told him about Murray's mutilated hand, I wasn't surprised at his lack of immediate pitying sounds. But I like a challenge, so I went on.

"Murray never cried about his hand," I told Bob. "He came to America with Florence, who he met somewhere over there, and had a family, namely, Joel. He was full of life, this Murray. He was a big drinker, he loved women, he beat his son with a strap, but he was a big personality."

Bob nodded.

I think the anti-Semite in him liked the "never cried" and "beat his son" parts of Murray. So I proceeded with my funeral story.

"I had lost touch with Joel for a few years. His wife threw him out for beating her and at least one of their daughters, and he was in one of his episodic 'hidings,' this time from the sheriff's department. They were after him for his house and all his earnings to give to his greedy wife. Somehow, I heard his father, Murray, had cancer and was dying. I called his mother and went over a few days later.

"We brought a bag of groceries, you know, French bread, a pound of sliced turkey, some wine, some vegetables, and a quart of milk. The usual stuff you bring when someone's sick, poor, and housebound. Florence and Joel greeted us at the door of their little one-bedroom apartment on Van Ness. I always liked it there, remembering the few Rosh Hashanah and Passover dinners they invited us to. Having been in the antiques business like my deceased father, Benny, the place was filled with oversized high-quality furniture and paintings. Murray was in a bathrobe in a gigantic English armchair, shrunken but beautiful in a way.

"He pulled me close and said, 'Michael, I remember when you took me and Joel to Chabad in Berkeley almost twenty years ago. I know you almost twenty years. That's not a short time. You took me to a bar after, on Telegraph. Those were the good times; now are the bad times.'

"Bob," I prodded, "you hear this? I extend one good deed twenty years ago, and this guy remembers. It's like one of the best moments of his life, this one good drink.

"So he goes fast into the hospital, where he insists they let him out, probably to die at home. And three or four days later, boom, it's over."

"Like that?"

"Joel told me he had been sick most of the night. Vomiting, probably those toxic chemo chemicals. He forces himself up and says, 'Joel, she's there. On your left, the angel of death.' Joel gets scared. He says, 'Pop, there's nobody here but me and Mom.' Murray stares at the big chair across the small room. 'To your right,

Joel. On the couch. He's here with her.' He stands up, starts to walk across the room, and collapses."

I can see that even the anti-Semite Bob is tearing up, wiping the tears from his face. "Listen, you racist," I said to him, "looking at that hole in the ground with Murray's casket so bare and hearing the rabbi's ancient chant and watching the young Mexican grave diggers moved by that chant, I became reminded of my own hole waiting.

"I never knew where I wanted to live," I whispered to Joel's friend from Israeli intelligence, "and I sure don't know where I want to die."

"We never know where we're going to die," he reminded me with a '70s-rocker's cackle and grin.

*There is that scattereth, and yet increaseth;
And there is that withholdeth more than is meet,
but it tendeth only to want.*

—Proverbs 11:24

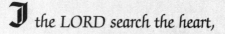

I the LORD search the heart,

I try the reins,

Even to give every man according to his ways,

According to the fruit of his doings.

— Jeremiah 17:10

The Savage Duality of Man: Animal Soul, Spiritual Soul

There is a war within each of us, due to the duality of the human soul. We are all both the transcendent spiritual man and the animal soul and we're in constant conflict. Our two souls have visions that oppose each other, and that makes many people crack up and think they're schizophrenic. And of course, most psychiatrists, God bless them, they're smart people, but not religious people, by and large. So they get it all wrong. If a person comes to them and says, "Oh, Doctor, I have two feelings about it, two thoughts about everything," their only answer is, "All right, here's medication."

In other words, "We'll kill one of your thoughts, and then you'll be a sane American." Then you can wind up having sex in the middle of the day on a rug or on the bare floor. You can use sex, drugs, and rock and roll. You'll be an ordinary American. In other words, a complete mess. But you won't be divided anymore.

So what is this mystical thing I'm trying to tell you? Do all religions teach this? I don't know about all religions. I don't see it in Buddhism. I don't think that Buddhists have ever been troubled by a duality of nature. I've read the Buddhist literature. It's beautiful poetry, and it tries to steer people on the right course, the right path of life. It does it through poetry and writings.

But mystical Jews have looked into and understand the animal soul and the spiritual soul. Though many believe that the two souls are opponents and you must suppress the animal soul, that's not what the teaching is. This is where Judaism differs from Christianity in its core philosophy. Judaism fundamentally differs from Christianity in that Judaism does not say to repress the animal soul. That's why some people say Jews are earthy people. Christians I've known have said this.

What they don't understand is that to achieve divinity, both souls, animal and spiritual, must equally spur this love for God. You must love your animal soul and turn it to the work of God. When the Talmud says to "love the Lord your God with all your heart," it means to love Him with both inclinations, both souls equally. It is our job or our challenge to transform the animal soul into an active partner in our divine service to God. The Talmud then explains how this transformation should occur.

When I talk about this subject on *The Savage Nation*, I can almost hear all the cynics in the audience saying, "Come on, cut the crap with the religion. I don't want to hear it. Stick to what you do, Mike. Get back to the humor. Stick to your politics. I don't believe in God. I don't believe in the soul." Okay, there's a cynical part of me, too. That's my animal soul. The cynical part of me that's mocking my own words, that's my animal soul mocking the godly side of me.

You can go crazy thinking about it all. I get it. I can hear my grandmother, the atheist, saying to me what she would say. My grandparents didn't believe in God. They really didn't. It's funny, I came from a family of atheists in many ways. My mother was religious but not religious. She wasn't religious, but she believed in God. She was afraid of God. I could see it in her eyes and in the things she did. She believed in God. She taught me about God. She had enough tragedy in her life to know that there had to be something more than life on this earth.

I think a lot of mental problems come from repression. The people who repress their thoughts or ideas most strongly become crazier. The more you try to repress what you're feeling, the more disturbed you become and the more violent you can become. So what am I saying? Why not do it in the road? Maybe there's a little truth to the hippie philosophy.

Watch where I'm going with this. I didn't say, "have sex whenever you feel like it." Here's the whole trick: to recognize that you have lust; to recognize that you have lust, if that's the issue for you. I'm giving you one example, sex, because that's all that we think about in America, day and night, sex, sex, sex, sex. Every newspaper you read, the eye goes to the right column, to every moron on a yacht in the Caribbean doing an Instagram upside down. Big deal. How many times can those bimbos stretch themselves on a rented boat to show us their bikinis?

Get over it, already. We all have a body. We've seen it all before. There are no ideas there. They're an example of the fallen man. It's sad for all those girls. They're like mental cases.

What I'm saying to you is don't repress what you're thinking and feeling. Accept what you're thinking and feeling, but don't act on it. I learned a long time ago that the trick is to recognize that you have those feelings but to refrain from acting on them. In one sentence, the difference between a sane person and an insane one is not what he thinks but what he does.

I had a caller on my radio show whose story was a perfect example of this. He told me that when he was a young college student, he didn't have any morals, any sense of what was truly right or wrong. He went to college and was confused sexually, which he associated with the animal side of man's nature. He ended up having a nervous breakdown and being diagnosed with paranoid schizophrenia. But, he said, finding God helped him deal with his underlying problems. It saved him.

According to the core, mystical beliefs of the Jewish people, not to be confused with the populist notion of a Jewish person, as exemplified by Woody Allen, but the deeply religious souls out there, you must harness the animal soul, not repress it or kill it. You must turn the animal soul over to the very same force as that of the godly soul.

My caller had learned to do that. And once he did, he was freed, emotionally, spiritually, and even sociopolitically. His life completely straightened out. He got a job, went back to school, and got good grades. And now, when he feels conflicted or ready to freak out, he prays. He asks God for help and asks friends for help. Finding God and getting control of his animal side not only saved him but gave him the tools to save himself in the future if he starts to wander off track.

I'm going to give you the kung fu of the truly insightful religious Jewish people, the ones you never meet, the ones you never see or hear. They talk about the greatness of God every day and say a prayer every day. It's called the *Shema Yisrael*, which means "God is one." And they relate to the spiritual source in the animal soul in the blessings that precede this prayer. So all the prayers of the Jewish people are about trying to harness both animal and spiritual selves together in a worship of God.

This is the thing people don't understand. What you see in religious people, whether they're Jewish or Christian or others, is not that they're pure because they think purely all the time. They have the same impulses that everybody has, but they don't act on them. They unify those powers or energies.

Knowing that helped me thirty years ago when I thought I was going to crack. I learned that the greater the animal soul and the more trouble it's causing you, the greater good you can do for the world. If you don't kill the animal soul but instead harness it to the better side of yourself and put it to work for the better side of yourself, you can do great work.

Harnessing the animal soul is what the Bible means by, "He moved mountains." It was from then on that I became what I am today. That is why I can speak to you every day on my radio show. As conflicted as I am, I can harness those forces and speak from Mount Sinai to my loyal audience on *The Savage Nation*.

And the dust returneth to the earth as it was,

And the spirit returneth unto God who gave it.

— Ecclesiastes 12:7

God Is Everywhere

God is not linear. God is infinite. Envision the Milky Way, all the stars and all the universes. All the pebbles, every grain of sand. All the crawling insects. God created all things, big and small. How we approach the Creator defines us.

Those who accept Jesus as the Son of God call themselves Christians. Those who bow to Allah are called Muslims. Jews worship the single entity they call God. What of Hindus, who worship not God but fantastic entities, and Buddhists, who read their poetry of life and bow down to an idol? What do we say of the many who worship the Great Spirit?

How do we define those who don't believe in an all-powerful God but may spend their conscious minutes pondering the stars and planets, the movements of celestial bodies, the quarks and sparks of dying stars millions of light years away? Or those who argue over causality, the physicists and scientists who say there is no God except for rational thought and electrical impulses that die when our bodies no longer emit signs of life? Are they not seeking the answer to this ancient riddle?

As Joel's friend said at the funeral, we never know where we're going to die. And we certainly don't know what comes next. In the meantime, we can look for the presence of God even here, amid all the ills of the world. In the end, the search to find God is the finding itself.

Acknowledgments

I want to thank my editor, Kate Hartson, for having the faith to publish this mysterious book. My agent, Ian Kleinert, for sticking with me during the white-water ride. Tom Mullen, for his excellent suggestions and organization of the biblical quotes. And those who so carefully worried over every comma.